This special edition of the Food Editors' Favorites: Treasured Recipes *is being offered to benefit MADD and help you better understand its work. Before enjoying the many recipes that follow, please take a few minutes to read over the material. It explains MADD's history and the services MADD performs. After reading these few pages, you will understand why MADD's work is so important and learn how you can support this worthwhile cause.*

It is estimated that two out of every five Americans will be involved in an alcohol-related crash in their lifetime. On average, 65 people die and 1,534 are injured each and every day as a result of alcohol and other drug-related driving crashes. Hopefully, through your support and involvement in the efforts of MADD, we can create a future that is less violent for us all.

Mothers Against Drunk Driving™

"Mothers Against Drunk Driving mobilizes victims and their allies to establish the public conviction that drunk driving is unacceptable and criminal, in order to promote corresponding public policies, programs and personal accountability."

MADD was founded in Fair Oaks, California in 1980. An aggressive campaign resulted in California passing the toughest drunk driving laws in the country at that time.

This astounding success on the West Coast was only the beginning. Shortly thereafter, MADD grew into a nationwide, non-profit corporation with more than one million members and supporters. Today, thousands of concerned citizens are active volunteers in over 385 chapters in 48 states. Affiliates are active in Canada, Australia, New Zealand and Great Britain. MADD is made up of both women and men who share a common concern for safety on our roads.

Numerous successes fuel the MADD operation, both at the National Office in Texas and in communities scattered throughout America. Since 1981, more than 950 drunk driving laws have been enacted nationwide. The rights of victims and survivors of alcohol related crashes are now being viewed more equitably in a criminal justice system which, only a few years ago, made the rights of the intoxicated driver a priority. Youth programs affiliated with MADD have sprung up in almost every state, providing teenagers with a sound background in alcohol awareness and education.

1

MADD's
Community Programs

MADD develops new ideas and programs to increase the unacceptability of drunk driving, and attempts to involve all Americans — especially our youth — in solving the problem. Some of our ongoing programs include:

Public Awareness Campaigns

Throughout the year, MADD conducts special campaigns to promote public awareness and raise the nation's consciousness of alcohol and other drug-impaired driving. These and other initiatives are MADD's most important tools for encouraging people to be responsible in their actions.

Project Red Ribbon: created by MADD to change the meaning of "tie one on" by asking drivers to tie a red ribbon to a visible location on their vehicles between Thanksgiving and New Year's Day. This is a simple but effective reminder to drive sober during the holiday season.

K.I.S.S. (Keep It a Safe Summer): spreads the word that summer months can be the most dangerous. A cornerstone of the program is the Family Vacation Pack, filled with safety tips and activities for the entire family!

Designated Driver: responsibility is the key to this program. The point: if you choose to drink, bring a friend who is not drinking to safely drive you home.

DRIVE FOR LIFE: is an annual public awareness campaign with one compelling goal...to save lives. MADD has selected one specific day—the Saturday of Labor Day Weekend—to focus increased education on the drunk driving issue. Citizens are asked to drive with their headlights on throughout that day in memory of the 65 men, women and children killed each day by drunk drivers and to sign a pledge not to drink and drive.

Candlelight Vigils: Each year MADD conducts Candlelight Vigils of Remembrance and Hope—remembrance of loved ones killed or injured in drunk driving crashes, and hope for a less violent future for us all.

Youth Education Programs

MADD has developed specific programs to reduce the prevalence of drinking and the incidence of drunk driving among America's youth. Components are designed to enhance student-parent dialogue, and to provide refusal skills training to show young people how to avoid dangerous situations involving alcohol and drug use.

Operation Prom/Graduation: This is a nationwide community awareness program that seeks to make prom and graduation nights memorable occasions, not memorial ones. Operation Prom/Graduation includes widespread drug-free activities and celebrations for students.

Nationwide Poster/Essay Contest: This national competition offers students in grades 1-12 the opportunity to exercise their creative writing and artistic skills to deliver a strong message about the dangers of drinking and driving. Individual entries compete at the National Office. The winners in each division then compete with organizational winners at the national level for awards and public recognition.

MADD Student Library: The Student Library is published annually to meet the needs of countless students who request information about teenage drunk driving. It contains statistics, case studies, articles on topics such as peer pressure and the legal aspects of teen drinking and an extensive bibliography of resources on highway safety issues. Educators and parents also regard it as a valuable resource.

Student Organizations: MADD offers guidance and detailed advice to high school students who are interested in organizing student groups to combat teenage impaired driving. Student leaders receive ideas for ongoing projects and programs to educate their peers and elevate their awareness about the disproportionate number of alcohol-related crashes caused by teenagers driving under the influence of alcohol and other drugs.

Friends Keep Friends Alive: MADD now offers an educational comic book directed at students in grades 4-9. The comic book teaches how to say no to drinking and drunk driving. It is offered in both English and Spanish.

FREE FOR LIFE: A refusal skills development program which teaches junior high school youth how to resist peer pressure to use alcohol and other drugs. The program relies on "peer education" techniques, having the students themselves plan and lead class discussions.

Speakers Bureaus

MADD chapters across America offer trained speakers to address civic and professional organizations, community groups, legislatures, public and private industries, schools and other concerned citizens. These knowledgeable leaders provide innovative lectures and educational information about critical traffic safety issues such as legislation, victims rights, community actions programs; and prevention techniques to remove intoxicated drivers from our highways.

Case / Court Monitoring

MADD's ongoing case/court monitoring program monitors the enforcement and legal process for DWI's in communities across America. Specifically, MADD volunteers monitor DWI arrests and cases being adjudicated in order to advise the public whether DWI laws, as well as enforcement, prosecution and defense are adequate.

MADD's
Legislative Goals

Since 1981, tremendous progress has been made at both the state and federal levels in passing tougher anti-drunk driving legislation. However, there is still much to do. This year, our legislative efforts will focus primarily on the following issues:

Victim Compensation. In keeping with the MADD objective of aiding victims of drunk driving crashes, MADD advocates that state governments provide a source of compensation funds for the financial losses and expenses of injured DWI victims and their families. At present, 36 states have established such programs, which provide crucial assistance for the victims who make application for funds.

Victim Bill of Rights. A Victim Bill of Rights provides a legislative means to ensure that victims of alcohol-related crashes have guaranteed rights within the criminal justice system. For many years such rights were disregarded in the effort to insure the rights of the accused, but it is increasingly recognized that the victim must also be accorded such protections as the right to describe the impact of the crime on his or her life and to be informed of developments in the adjudication process. In some states, a Bill of Rights has been established in comprehensive form, while in others, victim rights have been passed in individual laws. To date, 44 states have passed some version of a Victim Bill of Rights.

Administrative Revocation. Administrative license revocation is a procedure to suspend, at the time of arrest, the driving privileges of persons caught driving with an illegal concentration of alcohol in their bodies. Studies have shown that license suspension or revocation is one of the most effective sanctions in reducing subsequent crashes, and administrative revocation proves even more effective. By suspending the license at the time of the offense several objectives are accomplished: the impaired driver is subjected to the consequences of his/her actions immediately instead of six months or more later; the risk of repeat offenses and crashes is reduced; man hours are saved for both enforcement and adjudicative systems; and law enforcement morale often rises as efforts achieve more certain results. Currently 22 states and the District of Columbia have administrative revocation provisions.

License Plate Confiscation. Removing license plates from the vehicles of habitual drunk drivers or offenders who drive on suspended licenses serves to make those offenses more visible and the license sanctions more enforceable. Currently, one state has mandated this penalty for repeat offenders and 12 states have statutes permitting its use; other states are considering similar legislation.

Self-Sufficient Drunk Driving Programs Funded by Offenders. MADD supports efforts to provide funds for drunk driving programs through fees, fines and other assessments, both to ensure a reliable source of continuing funding for effective programs and to place the burden of these programs where it belongs: on the drunken driver.

Mandatory Alcohol/Drug Testing of all Drivers in Crashes Resulting in Fatalities/Serious Injury. MADD advocates the requirement of alcohol/drug testing of all drivers in all traffic crashes resulting in fatalities or serious bodily injury.

.08 Per Se / .05 Presumptive. In 41 states, a BAC level of .10 percent is considered "per se" evidence of intoxication; in many states a set level, usually .10 percent, is also considered to be "presumptive" evidence of intoxication. Research evidence shows that people are actually impaired at lower levels, and the American Medical Association has even called for a per se level of .05 percent. MADD supports making .08 per se evidence of intoxication with a presumptive level of .05. Currently three states have lowered the per se limit to .08.

Legislation Providing For Preliminary Breath Tests. MADD supports providing the most modern technology (Preliminary Breath Testers - PBTs) to police officers investigating drunken drivers, both to increase the efficiency of the arrest process and to protect the innocent.

Mandatory Incarceration for Repeat Offenders. MADD favors confinement which cannot be suspended or probated for those convicted more than once of driving while under the influence. Drunk driving is a crime, and continued incidence of such offenses warrants the punitive effect of a certain jail sentence. Making the sentence mandatory removes the uncertainty and increases deterrent value of the sanction.

Open Container. MADD supports laws which prohibit any occupant of a motor vehicle from possessing an open container of alcoholic beverage. Such a statute goes beyond the effect of "don't drink and drive" ordinances, under which an officer must actually observe the offense before an arrest may be made; such statutes make it easy for a driver to hand off his or her container to a passenger.

Dram Shop. Dram shop laws provide for lawsuits by alcohol-related crash victims against drinking establishments and individuals which serve alcoholic beverages irresponsibly to an intoxicated driver. At least 41 states have either case law or statutes concerning dram shop liability, although some of these provide specific limitations on the extent of liability.

Plastic Embossed Color-Coded Drivers' Licenses. The use of unalterable drivers' licenses which clearly indicate whether the driver is of drinking age is very important in enforcing the '21' drinking age law. Using a color code for under-drinking-age drivers facilitates identification, and utilizing a plastic-embossed license helps to forestall alteration of licenses.

Alcohol Warning Labels. MADD has endorsed the concept of requiring warning labels on alcoholic beverages stating that alcohol will impair skills necessary for operation of motor vehicles or heavy machinery. The use of such warnings is consistent with similar warnings on other hazardous substances and will provide a direct opportunity to educate the public concerning the risks involved in alcohol consumption.

MADD's
Victim Services

Each of the more than 23,600 fatalities and half a million serious injuries incurred yearly is a unique and irreplaceable individual with a name, a family, and dreams which must now go unfulfilled. Each represents far more than a faceless number to his or her family and friends, who are now caught in the tragic ripple effect set off by each crash.

For drunk driving victims — both injured persons and survivors of fatalities — MADD offers the following special services:

Crisis Intervention

Alcohol and other drug-related crashes create a critical period in the lives of victims. MADD provides emotional support to help victims cope with their grief and anger. In addition, victims receive practical information to help them understand the grieving process and their pending court cases.

Victim Support

MADD provides numerous reading materials to help victims understand their unique grieving symptoms. It also brings victims together in victim support groups to discuss their feelings and futures. Victims offer each other a unique understanding and provide emotional support and reassurance to those who share the loss or serious injury of a loved one.

Victim Advocacy

Victims are offered a thorough explanation of the judicial process. MADD advocates clarify the victims' rights, accompany them to court when necessary and follow-up on the sentencing of the offender. MADD offers the *Victim Information Pamphlet and Victims' Rights in Alcohol Impaired Crashes* to inform victims about their rights in court proceedings. The *MADDVOCATE* provides up-to-date information for victims and victim advocates.

Victim Impact Panels (VIPs)

Judges or probation officers order convicted drunk drivers to attend a Victim Impact Panel as a component of their sentencing. The panel is composed of three or four victims of drunk driving crashes who tell their stories simply and from the heart. The goal of the program is to enable the offenders to understand their crime from the victim perspective and choose to never again drink and drive.

Information and Referral

MADD chapters refer victims to state and local agencies which offer financial and legal information, as well as emotional assistance. Chapter members are always available to counsel and guide victims throughout the grieving process.

MADD
and You

Grassroots activism is the force of MADD. Your unyielding determination, commitment, energy, courage and creativity, along with thousands of others, is needed to reduce the number of deaths and injuries from alcohol & other drug-related driving.

You can help us create a future that is less violent for everyone. We invite you to become actively involved in the work to end alcohol & other drug-impaired driving. Together we can make a difference.

There are various ways to participate actively in this bold cause:

• Be responsible for your own thinking and actions about drunk driving—*don't drink and drive.*

• Support your family and friends in being responsible for their thinking and actions about drunk driving—*friends don't let friends drive drunk.*

• Be informed about the issues of drunk driving. Make yourself knowledgeable so that you can create conversations with others that raise their consciousness and support them in being responsible. MADD provides numerous written materials to educate you, and we are just a telephone call away.

• Be actively involved at whatever level you can give. If your community has a MADD chapter, make your talent and time available to help. Explore the possibility of organizing a chapter in your community, if one is not established. If you prefer, work with other resources in your community to fight alcohol & other drug-related driving, or create resources that are missing.

Thank you! Through your financial contribution, you have expressed a commitment to end alcohol & other drug-related driving. We hope you will take the next step and become actively involved. Contact MADD in your local community or the National Office.

MADD National Office
669 Airport Freeway, Suite 310
Hurst, Texas 76053
817/268-6233

Mothers Against Drunk Driving ™

7

FOOD EDITORS' FAVORITES

Treasured Recipes

Edited by
Barbara Gibbs Ostmann
and
Jane Baker
For
The Newspaper
Food Editors and Writers
Association, Inc.

This book was originally produced by and for the benefit of the Newspaper Food Editors and Writers Association, Inc. (NFEWA). NFEWA's permission to print this special edition of the book does not constitute an endorsement of MADD, nor is it intended to imply any relationship between NFEWA and MADD.

Library of Congress Cataloging in Publication Data
Main entry under title:
Food editors' favorite cookbook.
Includes index.
1. Cookery,   I. Baker, Jane.   II. Ostmann, Barbara
Gibbs. III. Newspaper Food Editors and Writers
Association (U.S.)
TX715.F67   1983   641.5 83-6199
ISBN 0-8437-3396-9 (pbk.)

Printed in the United States of America.

This special edition was published by Coupon Power, Inc.

10

Contents

Contributing Food Editors

Harriett Aldridge, *Arkansas Gazette*, Little Rock, AR
Donna Anderson, *Vancouver Sun*, Vancouver, British Columbia, Canada
Julian Armstrong, *The Gazette*, Montreal, Quebec, Canada
Bernie Arnold, *Nashville Banner*, Nashville, TN
Jane Baker, *The Phoenix Gazette*, Phoenix, AZ
Claire Barriger, Free-lance writer, Ottawa, Ontario, Canada
Kingsley Belle, *The Chronicle*, Glens Falls, NY
Bev Bennett, *Chicago Sun-Times*, Chicago, IL
Rosemary Black, *The Record*, Hackensack, NJ
Billie Bledsoe, *San Antonio Express and News*, San Antonio, TX
Marian Burros, *The New York Times*, New York, NY
Barbara Burtoff, Syndicated writer, Washington, DC
Ellen Carlson, *St. Paul Dispatch and Pioneer Press*, St.Paul, MN
Ivy Coffey, *El Reno Tribune*, El Reno, OK
Elaine Corn, *The Courier-Journal*, Louisville, KY
Joe Crea, *Florida Times-Union*, Jacksonville, FL
Ann Criswell, *Houston Chronicle*, Houston, TX
Jeanne Cummins, *Noblesville Daily Ledger*, Noblesville, IN
Beverly Daniel, *The Bellingham Herald*, Bellingham, WA
Peggy Daum, *The Milwaukee Journal*, Milwaukee, WI
Sue Dawson, *Columbus Dispatch*, Columbus, OH
Helen Dollaghan, *The Denver Post*, Denver, CO
Barbara Durbin, *The Oregonian*, Portland, OR
Sandal English, *Arizona Daily Star*, Tucson, AZ
Clara Eschmann, *The Macon Telegraph and News*, Macon, GA
Daisy Fitch, *Trenton Times*, Trenton, NJ
Vicki Fitzgerald, *The Patriot Ledger*, Quincy, MA
Janet Beighle French, *The Plain Dealer*, Cleveland, OH
Christine Arpe Gang, *The Commercial Appeal*, Memphis, TN
Linda Giuca, *The Hartford Courant*, Hartford, CT
Lorrie Guttman, *Tallahassee Democrat*, Tallahassee, FL
Carol Haddix, *Chicago Tribune*, Chicago, IL
Marilyn Hagerty, *Grand Forks Herald*, Grand Forks, ND
Deni Hamilton, *The Courier-Journal*, Louisville, KY
Phyllis Hanes, *The Christian Science Monitor*
Marge Hanley, *Indianapolis News*, Indianapolis, IN
Charlotte Hansen, *The Jamestown Sun*, Jamestown, ND
Natalie Haughton, *Daily News*, Van Nuys, CA
Susan Manlin Katzman, Free-lance writer, St. Louis, MO

Kathleen Kelly, *Wichita Eagle-Beacon*, Wichita, KS
Dorothy Kincaid, *Milwaukee Sentinel*, Milwaukee, WI
Alice Krueger, *Winnipeg Free Press*, Winnipeg, Manitoba, Canada
Pat Hanna Kuehl, *Rocky Mountain News*, Denver, CO
Donna Lee, *The Providence Journal and Bulletin*, Providence, RI
Kathy Lindsley, *Rochester Times-Union*, Rochester, NY
Jann Malone, *Richmond Times-Dispatch*, Richmond, VA
Karen K. Marshall, *St. Louis Globe-Democrat*, St. Louis, MO
Ann McDuffie, *The Tampa Tribune*, Tampa, FL
Barbara McQuade, *Vancouver Sun*, Vancouver, British Columbia, Canada
Cy Meier, *Thompson Newspapers of Upper Michigan*, Calumet, MI
Woodene Merriman, *Pittsburgh Post-Gazette*, Pittsburgh, PA
Nancy Millard, *Muncie Star*, Muncie, IN
Jane Milza, *Staten Island Advance*, Staten Island, NY
Donna Morgan, *Salt Lake Tribune*, Salt Lake City, UT
Joan Nathan, Free-lance writer, Chevy Chase, MD
Bernie O'Brien, *Hollywood Sun-Tattler*, Hollywood, FL
Janice Okun, *Buffalo News*, Buffalo, NY
Eleanor Ostman, *St. Paul Pioneer Press and Dispatch*, St.Paul, MN
Barbara Gibbs Ostmann, *St. Louis Post-Dispatch*, St. Louis, MO
Lou Pappas, *The Peninsula Times Tribune*, Palo Alto, CA
Nancy Pappas, *The Louisville Times*, Louisville, KY
Gail Perrin, *The Boston Globe*, Boston, MA
Anne Byrn Phillips, *The Atlanta Journal-Constitution*, Atlanta, GA
Mary Frances Phillips, *San Jose Mercury and News*, San Jose, CA
Mary Alice Powell, *The Blade*, Toledo, OH
Constance Quan, *The Village Gazette*, Old Greenwich, CT
Helen Wilber Richardson, *The Providence Journal and Bulletin*, Providence, RI
Phyllis Richman, *The Washington Post*, Washington, DC
Joyce Rosencrans, *The Cincinnati Post*, Cincinnati, OH
Marilyn McDevitt Rubin, *The Pittsburgh Press*, Pittsburgh, PA
Mary Scourtes, *The Tampa Tribune*, Tampa, FL
Donna Segal, *Indianapolis Star*, Indianapolis, IN
Mary Hart Sorenson, *Minneapolis Star and Tribune*, Minneapolis, MN
Elizabeth Sparks, *Winston-Salem Journal*, Winston-Salem, NC
Betty Straughan, *The News Review*, Roseburg, OR
Evelyn Wavpotich, *Island Packet*, Hilton Head Island, SC
Diane Wiggins, *St. Louis Globe-Democrat*, St. Louis, MO

Introduction

What do food editors discuss when they get together at conferences? In addition to such serious topics as nutrition, consumerism, government regulations and food prices, the discussion usually gets around to recipes and what's new in various areas.

As food editors, we have our fingers on the culinary pulse of cities across the country, even the world. We are continually exposed to all sorts of food: some good, some not so good. Sooner or later, we all end up with bulging personal recipe files.

The idea of putting food editors' favorite recipes into a cookbook was bound to come up. Sure enough, it did, and since 1978 we've been collecting personal favorites from our members to be shared with people everywhere via this cookbook.

We would like to make clear that these recipes are our favorites; we make no claim that they are original. (Is there really such a thing?) When possible, we've given credit where credit is due. But in many cases, recipes just evolved, and it is hard, if not impossible, to say from where they came.

This book is also our way of introducing the Newspaper Food Editors and Writers Association (NFEWA) to you. The association was founded in 1974 to encourage communication among food editors and writers, to foster professional ethical standards, to share our knowledge about food and to promote a greater understanding among other journalists.

Incorporated in 1982, the association has more than 150 members around the world, including the United States, Canada, New Zealand and Mexico. We sponsor an annual meeting with seminars, speakers and self-help sessions, as well as frequent regional meetings.

Perhaps the most important aspect of the association is the enthusiasm and support shared among the members, helping each other to continually strive to do a better job of serving the reader and the public.

We hope this book will find a special place in your own kitchen library, as it will in each of ours.

Jane Baker
Barbara Gibbs Ostmann
NFEWA

Appetizers

Crab Puffs

Barbara Durbin
The Oregonian, Portland, OR

A little crab goes a long way in this recipe. The puffs look fancy even though the preparation is simple.

Makes approximately 3 dozen appetizers

1 package (3 ounces) cream
cheese, softened
1/4 pound crab meat, fresh
canned or frozen
1 teaspoon finely minced garlic
Dash Worcestershire sauce
2 drops hot pepper sauce
1/4 teaspoon salt

1/8 teaspoon white pepper
1/2 pound (approx.) wonton
wrappers
Margarine
Vegetable oil for frying
Mustard powder
Water

Combine cream cheese, crab, garlic, Worcestershire, hot pepper sauce, salt and pepper.

Place 1/2 teaspoon (slightly rounded) crab filling in center of each wonton wrapper. Spread small amount margarine on two adjacent sides of wrapper. Fold one side over to form triangle. Press at edges to seal. (The margarine helps, since the wrappers are lightly floured and resist sticking.) Pinch in middle, then fold down opposite corners of triangle as though folding a paper airplane, forming wings.

Deep-fry in hot vegetable oil until golden. Drain on paper towels.

Serve with hot mustard made by mixing dry mustard powder and water to desired consistency.

Note: These can be assembled and refrigerated or frozen before frying. Be sure to keep them in an airtight container because the wonton skins dry out easily.

Curry Dip

Peggy Daum

The Milwaukee Journal, Milwaukee, WI

This curry dip served with vegetables has become my price of admission to many friends' parties. The original version of this recipe came from the home economists at the Wisconsin Gas Company as part of a food story on nutritious appetizers for New Year's Eve.

Makes approximately 2 cups

2 teaspoons curry powder
1-1/2 teaspoons garlic salt
2 tablespoons granulated sugar
2 teaspoons prepared
  horseradish
2 teaspoons grated onion

2 tablespoons cider vinegar
1 cup sour cream
1 cup mayonnaise
Cherry tomatoes
Raw vegetables in bite-size
  pieces

Mix curry powder, garlic salt, sugar, horseradish, onion and vinegar. Add sour cream and mayonnaise; mix well. Cover and chill several hours or overnight.

Serve with cherry tomatoes and bite-size pieces of other raw vegetables. Some of my favorites are cauliflower, broccoli, mushrooms, carrots, celery, green and red peppers, asparagus, kohlrabi and rutabaga.

Dill Dip In A Bread Bowl

Barbara Gibbs Ostmann
St.Louis Post-Dispatch, St. Louis, MO

This dill dip recipe appeared in my newspaper in a column written by Susan Manlin Katzman. It's easy to make, pretty to serve and delicious to eat. I serve it in a bread bowl, which is itself eaten.

Makes approximately 3 cups

1 large, round unsliced loaf Russian rye bread or other round loaf
1-1/3 cups sour cream
1-1/3 cups mayonnaise
2 tablespoons finely chopped fresh parsley

2 tablespoons grated onion
3 teaspoons chopped fresh dill leaf or 2 teaspoons dried dill weed (Do not use dill seed)
2 teaspoons Beau Monde seasoning (Available in most supermarkets)

With serrated knife, cut circle from center of bread, keeping sides intact; trim inside of bread to form bowl. Set bread bowl aside and cut remaining bread (part cut from center) into large, bite-size pieces. Set aside.

Combine sour cream, mayonnaise, parsley, onion, dill and Beau Monde. If you use dried dill weed, refrigerate dip overnight to let flavors develop and mingle.

Fill hollow portion of bread bowl with sour cream mixture just before serving. Place bread bowl on serving plate and surround it with cut bread pieces. Use bread as dippers.

Note: I usually double the amount of dip and use two loaves of bread, one for the "bowl" and the other to cut up in pieces. The dip is also good with assorted raw vegetables.

Hot Mushroom Sandwiches
Barbara Burtoff
Syndicated writer, Washington, D.C.

When Helen Gurley Brown, editor of Cosmopolitan, entertains, she turns over the cooking to "one wonderful caterer" and concentrates on her guest list. "I work fiendishly hard about whom to combine. I like to have somebody interesting at each party, but I don't bring in someone from Mars. I mix up up people who have quite a lot in common but don't know each other, although each guest should know at least two others besides the host and hostess," she said. This party hors d'oeuvre recipe, one of Ms. Brown's favorites, was shared by New York City caterer, Donald Bruce White.

Makes 21 sandwiches

1-1/2 cups finely minced
   fresh mushrooms
1 tablespoon thinly minced
   shallots or whites of
   scallions (green onions)
4 tablespoons butter, divided
3 tablespoons all-purpose flour
1/2 cup chicken stock

1/2 cup heavy cream
Dash cayenne
Dash ground nutmeg
Dash salt
Dash white pepper
21 slices firm white bread,
   sliced thin

Mince mushrooms and shallots. Sauté in 2 tablespoons butter. Allow liquid from mushrooms to cook down.

Melt remaining 2 tablespoons butter in separate pan; stir in flour to make roux (paste). Add chicken stock, cream, cayenne, nutmeg, salt and white pepper. Cook until mixture becomes quite thick. (Don't let heat get too high.) When mixture is thick, add mushroom mixture.

Trim crusts from bread. Spread some mushroom mixture on one slice of bread, add second slice, more mushroom mixture, then add third and final slice of bread. Don't spread mushroom mixture to edges, or it will ooze out. (There should be enough mushroom mixture to make 7 triple-decker sandwiches.)

Preheat oven or toaster-oven to 400°F. Toast sandwiches 10 to 12 minutes, or until they are slightly golden in color. Cut each sandwich into three fingers and serve warm.

Note: These sandwiches could also be served for lunch or as part of a tea menu.

Love Letters

Karen K. Marshall

St. Louis Globe-Democrat, St. Louis, MO

*I developed this recipe for a dinner that was sold at a
local charity auction one year. The host paid $900 for
the dinner, which I cooked for ten people; I thought he
deserved something just a little different.*

Makes 4-1/2 to 5 dozen appetizers

2 cups shredded cooked
   chicken
1 can (4 ounces) chopped
   green chilies, drained
4 large green onions, finely
   chopped
1/3 cup grated Parmesan cheese

Dash each garlic powder and
   onion powder
Dash salt
1 package (16 ounces) wonton
   wrappers
Vegetable oil for frying

Combine chicken, chilies, green onions, cheese, garlic and onion powders and salt in medium-size bowl; mix well.

Place a wrapper on counter with one corner facing toward you. Put about 1 teaspoon chicken mixture slightly below center of wrapper and fold bottom corner up. Fold sides in, points overlapping. Wet edges to seal. Fold final corner down, to resemble an envelope. Wet edges slightly to seal. Repeat with remaining chicken and wrappers.

Deep-fry, a few at a time, until golden and crispy around edges. Drain on paper towels; serve hot.

Note: Love Letters are good plain, but they are also good served with sour cream and/or sweet-sour sauce.

These freeze beautifully. To prevent sticking, spread uncooked wontons on cookie sheets and set in freezer just until hard. Do not thaw before frying. If desired, they can be fried several hours before guests arrive; simply reheat in a 400°F. oven for 5 to 10 minutes.

Olive-Cheese Balls
Beverly Daniel
The Bellingham Herald, Bellingham, WA

Makes approximately 36 appetizers

2 cups finely grated Cheddar
  cheese
1/2 cup butter, softened
1/4 teaspoon hot pepper sauce
1/2 teaspoon salt

1 teaspoon paprika
1 cup all-purpose flour,
  unsifted
36 pimiento-stuffed green
  olives (approx.)

Mix thoroughly cheese, butter, hot pepper sauce, salt, paprika and flour. Form portion of dough around each well-drained olive. Bake in 400°F. oven about 15 minutes, or until golden brown.

Note: These cheese balls can be made ahead and frozen, then popped in the oven and cooked just before serving.

Bowknots
Kathleen Kelly
Wichita Eagle-Beacon, Wichita, KS

Makes 2 dozen appetizers

1 loaf fresh sandwich bread
  (white or whole wheat),
  thinly sliced
1 can (10-1/2 ounces)
  condensed cream of
  mushroom soup, undiluted

12 bacon strips, uncooked, cut
  in half
24 toothpicks

Trim all crust off bread. Spread soup on one side of bread slices, being careful to cover edges. Roll each slice from one corner to opposite corner. Wrap bacon strip around middle of each roll and secure with toothpick. Place on cookie sheet and bake in 250°F. oven for 1 hour. The bowknots will be dry, crisp and delicious.

Note: Prepared bowknots may be frozen before baking. Place on a flat pan; when frozen solid, transfer to freezer bags. Bake without thawing, extending baking time about 15 minutes.

Other condensed soups such as cream of asparagus or chicken can be substituted for the mushroom soup.

Spinach Frittata

Lou Pappas

The Peninsula Times Tribune, Palo Alto, CA

This vegetable-strewn omelet is excellent as an appetizer when cut into squares or diamonds. Cut in large rectangles, it makes an excellent accompaniment to an entrée.

Makes 6 dozen appetizers

4 bunches green onions (approx. 24), finely chopped
4 tablespoons butter
2 bunches (approx. 2 pounds) spinach, finely chopped
1/3 cup finely chopped fresh parsley
12 eggs
1/2 teaspoon salt
1/4 teaspoon freshly ground pepper
1/8 teaspoon ground nutmeg (optional)
1/2 cup sour cream
1-1/2 cups shredded Gruyère, Swiss or Cheddar cheese
3/4 cup shredded Parmesan cheese, divided

Sauté the onions in butter until tender in large frying pan. Add spinach and sauté 2 minutes. Remove from heat; add parsley, then set aside.

Beat eggs in bowl until light; mix in salt, pepper, nutmeg, sour cream, shredded cheese, half the Parmesan cheese and the onion mixture. Pour into well-greased 15x10x1-inch jelly roll pan. Sprinkle with remaining Parmesan cheese.

Bake in preheated 350°F. oven 25 minutes, or until set. Cut into squares or diamonds. Serve hot.

Curried Chicken Roll-Ups

Alice Krueger

Winnipeg Free Press, Winnipeg, Manitoba, Canada

This appetizer goes over well with guests because it's refreshingly light.

Makes 2 dozen appetizers

4 chicken breast halves
2 cups chicken broth or bouillon
3 to 4 teaspoons curry powder
24 lettuce leaves (leaf or
   butter type)

1 cup sour cream
3 tablespoons finely chopped,
   toasted sunflower seeds
1/4 cup finely chopped chutney
1 cup toasted coconut

Combine chicken breasts, broth and curry powder in medium-size saucepan. Bring to boil and simmer 30 minutes, or until chicken is tender. Remove from heat; refrigerate without draining, allowing chicken to cool in broth for several hours. In the meantime, wash lettuce leaves and pat dry.

Remove chicken breasts from broth; remove and discard skin and bones. Cut each half-breast into 6 to 8 fingers, each 2 to 3 inches in length and 1/2 inch wide. Place each strip of chicken on lettuce leaf; fold in sides of leaf and roll up. Secure with toothpick, if necessary. Refrigerate rolls for several hours before serving.

Dip for rolls: Combine sour cream, sunflower seeds and chutney. Refrigerate until serving time.

Arrange chicken rolls on large platter or tray with dip and toasted coconut in small bowls in center. To serve, dunk rolls in dip, then in coconut.

Egg-Shrimp Divine

Marilyn Hagerty

Grand Forks Herald, Grand Forks, ND

*Sometimes the things that are the easiest to make are
the most elegant. This is one of those recipes.*

Makes approximately 2 cups

1 package (8 ounces) cream
cheese
3 tablespoons mayonnaise
1/2 teaspoon curry powder
1 can (6 ounces) shrimp,
drained

1 hard-cooked egg, chopped
1/4 cup chopped green onions
1 tablespoon finely chopped
celery
Paprika
Crackers

Mix cream cheese with mayonnaise and curry powder; beat until smooth. Press into shallow soup bowl. Mix thoroughly shrimp, egg, onions and celery. Press shrimp mixture into cheese mixture. Sprinkle with paprika. Chill to blend flavors.

Serve with crackers.

Lime Fruit Dip

Donna Morgan

Salt Lake Tribune, Salt Lake City, UT

Makes approximately 2 cups

2 eggs
1/2 cup granulated sugar
4 teaspoons cornstarch
1 can (6 ounces) frozen limeade
concentrate, undiluted

2 to 3 drops green food coloring
1 cup heavy cream, whipped
Fresh fruit, cut into sticks, and
berries

Beat eggs and combine in top of double boiler with sugar, cornstarch and limeade concentrate. Cook until thickened, stirring frequently. Remove from heat and stir in food coloring. Cool. Whip cream and fold into cooled limeade mixture.

Transfer to bowl or individual serving dishes and serve with fresh fruit and berries.

Note: This mixture can be frozen, but it also keeps well in the refrigerator.

Eggplant Appetizer

Jane Baker

The Phoenix Gazette, Phoenix, AZ

This is great party fare. It's easy to make and can be prepared ahead of time. The only problem is there are never any leftovers—it's too good. I originally found the recipe in an Italian cookbook, but "perfected" it with different ingredients.

Makes 4 to 8 servings

1/4 cup olive oil
1 onion, chopped
4 cloves garlic, minced
1 medium eggplant, peeled and chopped
2 green peppers, seeded and chopped
1 cup chopped celery
1 can (8 ounces) pitted black olives, drained and chopped

1 cup chopped mushrooms
1 can (8 ounces) tomato sauce
2 tablespoons wine vinegar
1/4 cup light brown sugar
1/4 teaspoon basil, crushed
Salt and pepper to taste
Italian bread, cut into thick slices or cubes

Heat olive oil in large, heavy skillet. Add onion and garlic; sauté until tender. Add eggplant, green pepper and celery. Cook, covered, stirring occasionally, for about 15 minutes. Add olives, mushrooms and tomato sauce; mix thoroughly. Add vinegar, brown sugar and basil; simmer uncovered until all ingredients are tender, about 15 minutes. Season with salt and pepper to taste.

Serve at room temperature with Italian bread, or refrigerate until needed. This also can be served warm as a vegetable dish.

Gougère Bourgignon

Constance Quan
The Village Gazette, Old Greenwich, CT

Gougère is a light, ring-shaped pastry with a delicate cheese flavor. It is native to the Burgundy region of France, from which come many fine wines. Traditionally, gougère is served at wine tastings to clear the palate between samplings. It is equally enjoyable as an hors d' oeuvre at a holiday cocktail party or afternoon tea.

1 cup sifted all-purpose flour	1 teaspoon salt
1/2 cup water	3 eggs
2 tablespoons unsalted butter	1/4 cup grated Gruyère cheese

Measure flour and set aside. Put water, butter and salt into saucepan. Bring water to full rolling boil, letting butter melt completely. Remove from heat. Immediately add flour and mix thoroughly, using heavy wooden spoon.

Beat 2 eggs; add gradually to flour mixture, beating well after each addition. When mixture is well blended, put into pastry bag with medium plain tip.

Pipe mixture onto baking sheet, forming 6-inch circle. Pipe concentric second circle just slightly larger, touching first circle. Pipe third circle on top of first two circles, resting between them. (As they bake, the three rings will fuse into one.)

Beat third egg. Use pastry brush to gently brush some beaten egg on top circle. Sprinkle cheese over egg-glazed surface. Bake in preheated 425°F. oven 25 minutes, or until puffed, golden and slightly dry. Serve warm or cool.

Holiday Antipasto

Janet Beighle French
The Plain Dealer, Cleveland, OH

This antipasto has earned a permanent place at my annual Christmas bash—a snack buffet for about 100 people. I alter it from year to year. This is the current version.

Makes approximately 3-1/2 quarts

1 bottle (8 ounces) Italian salad dressing
4 cups sliced carrots
2 cups coarsely diced onion
1 cup sliced celery
1 cup sliced mushrooms
1 can (14 ounces) artichoke hearts, drained

1 jar (11 ounces) baby eggplants, drained
1 cup Greek olives, drained and pitted
1 jar (15-1/2 ounces) dilled Brussels sprouts or broccoli
2 jars (2 ounces each) chopped pimiento

Heat Italian dressing in large skillet. Add carrots; cover and cook 5 minutes. Add onion, celery and mushrooms; stir. Cover and cook 5 minutes longer. Vegetables should be hot through, but still colorful and crisp. Celery will eventually fade in color.

Uncover and let cool. Chill. Add artichokes, eggplants, olives, Brussels sprouts or broccoli and pimiento. Chill until serving time.

Note: This recipe keeps at least a week in the refrigerator.

Dilled tomatoes can be used in place of the Brussels sprouts or broccoli. The dilled vegetables should be easily obtainable at a Greek grocery.

Mimi's Artichoke Squares

Barbara Durbin

The Oregonian, Portland, OR

Many recipes that have become my favorites came from people I have written about in the newspaper through the years. This recipe for Artichoke Squares is one example. It goes together fast with a food processor to chop the onion and artichoke and to make the bread crumbs and shred cheese

Makes 3 dozen appetizers

2 jars (6 ounces each) marinated artichokes
1 onion, finely chopped
2 cloves garlic, crushed
4 eggs
1/4 cup fine dry bread crumbs
1/4 teaspoon salt
1/8 teaspoon pepper
1/8 teaspoon oregano
1/8 teaspoon hot pepper sauce
2 cups grated sharp Cheddar cheese
2 tablespoons (or more) minced fresh parsley

Drain marinade from 1 jar of artichokes into skillet. Drain second jar of artichokes. Chop artichokes; set aside. Add onion and garlic to marinade in skillet. Sauté until limp, about 5 minutes.

Beat eggs in bowl; add bread crumbs, salt, pepper, oregano and hot pepper sauce. Stir in cheese, parsley, artichokes and onion mixture. Pour into greased 11x7x2-inch baking pan. Bake in 325°F. oven for 30 minutes, or until set.

Let cool, then cut into squares. Serve cold or reheat in 325°F. oven for 10 to 12 minutes.

Note: The marinade from the second jar of artichokes can be reserved for use as a salad dressing.

Mushroom Appetizers

Donna Anderson
Vancouver Sun, Vancouver, British Columbia, Canada

Makes 2 dozen appetizers

24 thin bread slices, crusts removed, buttered on both sides
4 tablespoons butter
3 shallots, chopped
1 pound fresh mushrooms, chopped fine
2 tablespoons all-purpose flour
1 cup heavy cream
1 tablespoon Dijon mustard
1/2 teaspoon salt
1/8 teaspoon cayenne
1 tablespoon chopped fresh parsley or 1 teaspoon crushed dried parsley
1-1/2 tablespoons chopped chives
2 teaspoons lemon juice

Grease small muffin tins (total 24 muffins); fit one bread slice into each mold. Trim edges of bread as necessary. Bake in 400°F. oven 10 minutes. Remove bread shells from muffin tins and cool on rack.

Melt butter in skillet and sauté shallots for a few minutes. Add mushrooms and cook, stirring often, until all moisture has gone. Stir in flour until well blended; add cream and cook, stirring, until thickened. Add mustard, salt, cayenne, parsley, chives and lemon juice, stirring to blend. Place cooled shells on cookie sheet and fill with mushroom mixture. Bake in 350°F. oven 10 minutes. Allow to cool slightly before serving.

Note: The unfilled bread shells may be frozen. It is not necessary to thaw them before filling with the mushroom mixture. The mushroom mixture may be made a day or two ahead of time.

Salmon Roll

Marilyn Hagerty
Grand Forks Herald, Grand Forks, ND

Tina and Earl Isaacson, who now spend most of their time in Bradenton, Florida, were among the most hospitable people who ever lived in Grand Forks. This is one of Tina's recipes.

Makes approximately 2 cups

1 can (16 ounces) red salmon
1/2 cup chopped pecans
1 package (8 ounces) cream
  cheese, softened

3 tablespoons chopped fresh
  parsley
2 drops liquid smoke or
  Worcestershire sauce
Crackers

Combine salmon, cream cheese and liquid smoke or Worcestershire; mix well. Shape into ball or log. Roll in mixture of pecans and parsley. Roll up in plastic wrap or wax paper. Chill to blend flavors. Serve with crackers.

Zippy Cheese Ball

Barbara Durbin
The Oregonian, Portland, OR

There are enough cheese ball recipes to fill volumes. But this one, though it may appear as unremarkable as the next, has enough zip to make it disappear quickly at parties.

3 cups shredded Cheddar cheese
1 package (8 ounces) cream
  cheese, softened
2 tablespoons mayonnaise

2 tablespoons Worcestershire
  sauce
1-1/2 teaspoons onion powder
Chopped nuts
Crackers or fresh vegetables

Mix thoroughly Cheddar cheese, cream cheese, mayonnaise, Worcestershire and onion powder. Blend well. Form into large ball. Roll in chopped nuts.

Serve with crackers or fresh vegetables.

Summary Crab Mold

Susan Manlin Katzman
Free-lance writer, St. Louis, MO

This is my husband's favorite appetizer. I wanted to call the dish "Crab Marshall" after him, but feared he would find the name a dubious compliment.

Makes 16 to 20 servings

1/4 cup butter
1/4 cup all-purpose flour
1-1/4 cups milk
1 package (8 ounces) cream cheese
1 envelope unflavored gelatin
3 tablespoons water
3/4 cup mayonnaise
2/3 cups chopped celery

1 cup canned or frozen crab meat, chopped and cleaned
1 small onion, grated
Beau Monde seasoning (Available in most supermarkets) to taste
Salt to taste
Hot pepper sauce to taste
Sesame seed crackers

Melt butter in saucepan and whisk in flour. Cook, stirring constantly, 1 minute. Gradually whisk in milk to make white sauce. When thickened, stir in cream cheese. Soften gelatin in water and add to hot mixture; stir to dissolve gelatin. Remove mixture from heat.

Stir in mayonnaise, celery, crab and onion. Add Beau Monde, salt and hot pepper sauce to taste.

Rinse 4- to 5-cup mold with cold water. Fill mold with crab mixture and chill until firm. Unmold and serve with sesame crackers.

Sweet And Sour Meatballs

Barbara Burtoff
Syndicated writer, Washington, D.C.

*For many years, Mildred Albert, now in her seventies,
owned the Hart Modeling Agency in Boston and had
cause to entertain many international celebrities from
the fashion world. No matter how elaborate a menu was
presented by a local caterer, guests could always count
on these scrumptious Sweet and Sour Meatballs (Ms.
Albert's own specialty) being on the hors d'oeuvre
table. As proof of their popularity, the meatballs were
always the first dish to disappear.*

Makes 75 to 85 meatballs

1 clove garlic, minced
2 pounds ground beef
2 eggs
3 tablespoons chili sauce
2 tablespoons dried parsley
  flakes
1/2 teaspoon salt
1/2 teaspoon pepper, divided

1 quart (32 ounces) cocktail
  vegetable juice
1 box (1 pound) light brown
  sugar
1 cup white vinegar
3 cloves garlic, halved
30 prunes, pitted

Mash minced garlic with ground beef, eggs, chili sauce, parsley flakes, salt and 1/4 teaspoon pepper. Shape meat mixture into 75 to 85 balls.

Combine vegetable juice, brown sugar, vinegar, garlic cloves and remaining pepper; bring mixture to boil.

Drop meatballs into juice mixture. Reduce heat to low; cook 40 minutes. Add prunes; cook 20 minutes more.

Drain off most, but not all, sauce before putting meatballs and prunes into chafing dish. Serve hot with toothpicks.

Note: A quart is 32 ounces, if you buy the 46-ounce can of cocktail vegetable juice, do not use the whole thing.

It is best to make these a day ahead, then refrigerate them. At serving time, you can skim off the fat on top of mixture before reheating.

To make 115 to 125 meatballs, increase the meat mixture ingredients by half; leave the sauce ingredients as they are.

Shrimp Spread

Jane Baker
The Phoenix Gazette, Phoenix, AZ

Makes approximately 6 cups

1 can (10-1/2 ounces)
condensed tomato soup,
undiluted
1 package (8 ounces) cream
cheese, softened
1-1/2 tablespoons unflavored
gelatin
2 tablespoons water
1 cup mayonnaise

1 tablespoon Worcestershire
sauce
Hot pepper sauce to taste
2 cans (4-1/2 ounces each)
shrimp, drained
1/2 cup chopped celery
1/2 cup chopped onion
Lettuce leaves
Crackers

Bring undiluted soup to boil in medium saucepan. Remove from heat and add cream cheese; stir until smooth. Soften gelatin in water. Add to hot soup mixture and stir until gelatin is dissolved. Add mayonnaise, Worcestershire and hot pepper sauce; mix well.

Refrigerate until slightly thickened. Add shrimp, celery and onion; mix well. Pour into lightly oiled 6-cup ring mold or other 6-cup gelatin mold. Refrigerate until firm.

Unmold onto platter lined with lettuce leaves. Serve with party crackers.

Note: The shrimp mixture also can be divided among several smaller molds to facilitate serving at large parties.

Vegetable Hot Dip

Donna Morgan
Salt Lake Tribune, Salt Lake City, UT

Makes approximately 1-1/2 cups

4 medium tomatoes, finely
  chopped
1/2 onion, finely chopped
1/2 cup finely chopped celery
1/4 cup finely chopped
  green pepper

2 tablespoons chopped green
  chilies
2 tablespoons red wine vinegar
1/4 cup vegetable oil
1 teaspoon mustard seed
Salt and pepper to taste
Corn chips or raw vegetables

Combine tomatoes, onion, celery, green pepper, chilies, vinegar, oil, mustard seed, salt and pepper. Allow mixture to chill at least 2 hours before serving. If you like a hotter dip, add more chopped green chilies.

Serve with corn chips or an assortment of raw vegetables such as celery, carrots, mushrooms or green pepper.

Soups

Beefy Vegetable Soup

Karen K. Marshall

St. Louis Globe-Democrat, St. Louis, MO

We call this Mom's Presbyterian version of chicken soup. Although it can be made with a hearty stock and hunks of beef, this version is quicker and, I think, just as good.

Makes approximately 6 quarts

2 to 3 carrots, chopped
2 large potatoes, chopped
1 large onion, chopped
4 ribs celery, preferably with tops, chopped
1 small head cabbage, coarsely shredded (approx. 3 cups)

1 to 2 pounds ground beef
2 teaspoons salt
1 teaspoon freshly ground pepper
1 quart tomato juice

Combine carrots, potatoes, onion, celery, cabbage, ground beef, salt and pepper in large stock pot and add enough water to cover. Add tomato juice. Bring to boil, then lower heat and simmer at least 1 hour, until meat is cooked and vegetables are tender. Stir occasionally to break up meat. Skim off fat and taste for seasoning.

Note: This soup freezes beautifully and generally tastes better the second or third day. The amounts of ingredients are flexible, but all of the ingredients should be fresh.

Butternut Squash Soup
Phyllis Hanes
The Christian Science Monitor

Makes 6 to 8 servings

1 medium butternut squash (approx. 1 pound)
3 tart green apples, peeled and coarsely chopped
1 medium onion, peeled and chopped
1/4 teaspoon rosemary or marjoram (optional)
1 teaspoon salt
1/4 teaspoon pepper
3 cans (10-1/2 ounces each) chicken broth
2 soup cans of water
1/4 cup heavy cream or half-and-half
Chopped fresh parsley for garnish

Peel squash and seed it; cut into chunks. Combine squash with apples, onions, rosemary, salt, pepper, broth and water in large, heavy saucepan. Bring to boil and simmer, uncovered, for 45 minutes.

Purée soup in blender or food processor. Return mixture to saucepan and bring just to boiling point, then reduce heat. Before serving, add cream. Serve hot, with chopped fresh parsley sprinkled on top.

Zucchini Soup
Marilyn Hagerty
Grand Forks Herald, Grand Forks, ND

When summer melts into September, the days grow cooler and you have more zucchini than you know how to handle. Here's a simple, super zucchini soup. It's almost too easy to believe — and it is low in calories.

Makes approximately 4 servings

2 cups sliced zucchini
2 cups water
3 chicken bouillon cubes
1 cup milk

Add sliced zucchini to combined water and bouillon cubes in saucepan. Heat until zucchini is tender. Pour mixture into blender or food processor and pureé. Return puréed mixture to pan and add milk. Heat to serving temperature.

Chilled Cucumber Soup

Donna Segal

Indianapolis Star, Indianapolis, IN

This soup tastes fantastic after we have spent an afternoon in the sun. I also like to serve it in cups, as the first course for a dinner party, and my daughters like it for between-meal snacking.

Makes 4 to 6 servings

2 tablespoons butter or margarine
1/2 cup chopped green onion, including some tops
2 cups diced seeded cucumber (approx. 1 large cucumber)
1 cup watercress or leaf spinach, chopped

1/2 cup peeled and diced potato (approx. 1 medium potato)
2 cups chicken broth
3/4 teaspoon salt
1/2 teaspoon white pepper
1 cup light or heavy cream
Thinly sliced radishes for garnish

Melt butter in saucepan; add green onion and cook over moderate heat for 5 minutes, being sure not to brown butter or onions. Add cucumber, watercress, potato, broth, salt and pepper; bring to boil. Reduce heat to low and cook for 15 minutes, or until vegetables are tender. Cool slightly.

Purée in blender, adding 1-1/2 cups of mixture at a time. Put in large bowl and stir in cream; cover and chill thoroughly for several hours or overnight.

When ready to serve, float several thin radish slices atop each serving.

Note: Other garnishes might be a sprinkle of paprika or curry powder, chopped chives or a cucumber slice.

Gazpacho

Mary Hart Sorensen
Minneapolis Star and Tribune, Minneapolis, MN

This recipe came from a reader more than fifteen years ago and is the most filling and delicious gazpacho I have ever consumed.

Makes 10 servings

1 small clove garlic, chopped
and mashed
1 tablespoon granulated sugar
1-1/2 teaspoons salt
1 can (46 ounces) tomato juice
1/4 cup vegetable oil
2 tablespoons lemon juice
1 teaspoon Worcestershire
sauce

3 tomatoes, finely chopped
1 cucumber, peeled and diced
1 green pepper, finely diced
1 cup shredded carrots
1 cup thinly sliced celery
1/4 cup thinly sliced green
onion

Combine garlic, sugar, salt, tomato juice, oil, lemon juice and Worcestershire in large bowl. Beat until well blended. Stir in tomatoes, cucumber, green pepper, carrots, celery and green onion. Cover and chill for several hours.

Note: This keeps 3 to 4 days in the refrigerator. Calories can be cut by eliminating the vegetable oil. The texture will not be as thick, but the flavor will not be impaired.

Brown Mushroom Soup

Jeanne Cummins
Noblesville Daily Ledger, Noblesville, IN

This recipe came from a native Parisian whom I met in Canada. It uses mature, brown mushrooms that give off a rich woodsy taste and often can be purchased at reduced prices.

Makes approximately 6 servings

1 pound mature (Mature mushrooms are dry, not slimy) mushrooms, diced
1/2 cup diced celery
1/2 cup diced carrots

1/4 cup diced onion
3 cups water (approx.)
Rich chicken or beef stock
Salt and pepper to taste

Cover mushrooms, celery, carrots and onion with water in 2- quart saucepan. Simmer, partially covered, for about 45 minutes. Add stock to make 6 cups of liquid. Add salt and pepper to taste. Heat through.

Chilled Blueberry Soup

Diane Wiggins
St. Louis Globe-Democrat, St. Louis, MO

My husband refused to eat cold soup. "Soup should be hot!" is his idea. After coaxing him into tasting this recipe, he polished off two bowls.

Makes 8 servings

3 cups water
1 quart fresh blueberries, rinsed, stemmed and drained
3/4 cup granulated sugar
Ground cinnamon to taste

2 tablespoons cornstarch
1-1/2 to 2 tablespoons cold water
Sour cream or yogurt for garnish

Bring water to boil in saucepan. Add blueberries, sugar and cinnamon. Cook for several minutes, stirring to dissolve sugar. Set aside. In small bowl mix cornstarch with enough cold water to make paste. Stir into warm berry mixture and bring to boil again. Cool. Cover and refrigerate. Serve well chilled with tablespoon of sour cream or yogurt atop each bowl of soup. Sprinkle with additional cinnamon.

Minestrone Siciliano

Natalie Haughton
Daily News, Van Nuys, CA

This Italian favorite—an array of fresh vegetables in beef stock seasoned to perfection — will rate rave reviews.

Makes approximately 3 quarts

1 to 1-1/2 pounds beef bones or small piece of beef chuck
2 teaspoons seasoned salt
6 cups water
1 can (15 ounces) butter beans, undrained
1 cup fresh green beans, cut in 1/2-inch slices, or 1 package (9 ounces) frozen green beans
3 medium carrots, peeled and diced
1 large potato, peeled and diced

2 medium tomatoes, coarsely chopped
1 small onion, chopped
1 tablespoon chopped fresh parsley
1-1/2 teaspoons dried basil
Freshly ground pepper to taste
1 small head cabbage, chopped
1 package (10 ounces) frozen peas, partly thawed
1 large zucchini, sliced

Combine beef bones, seasoned salt, water, beans, carrots, potato, tomatoes, onion, parsley, basil and pepper in large soup pot. Cover and heat to boiling; reduce heat and add cabbage. Cover and simmer 1 hour.

Remove bones from soup, cut off any meat and return meat to soup. Stir in peas and zucchini; simmer 5 to 10 minutes longer.

Cream of Fall-Vegetable Soup

Daisy Fitch
Trenton Times, Trenton, NJ

This is a lovely rose-colored soup that is delicately flavored with herbs and curry power.

Makes 6 servings

3 small beets, peeled and chopped
3 green onions, sliced
2 small yellow onions, chopped
3 carrots, peeled and sliced
1 potato, peeled and cubed
2 ribs celery, sliced
1/2 cup chopped fresh parsley

3-1/2 cups chicken broth
2 teaspoons butter
2 teaspoons all-purpose flour
1 cup light cream or half-and-half
1/2 teaspoon curry powder
1/2 teaspoon salt

Combine beets, green and yellow onion, carrots, potato, celery, parsley and chicken broth in large saucepan. Cover and simmer for 25 minutes, or until potatoes and carrots are tender. Whirl in blender or food processor in batches until ingredients are minced, but not too smooth.

Melt butter in another large saucepan. Add flour and cook, stirring 1 minute. Add cream and cook, stirring with wire whisk until just at boiling point. Add vegetable mixture, curry powder and salt. Heat through.

Salads

German Potato Salad

Karen K. Marshall

St. Louis Globe-Democrat, St. Louis, MO

This is a party-size potato salad, but it is easily reduced in size. You can make it a day ahead, but it suffers if made any sooner than that.

Makes 20 to 25 servings

6 pounds new potatoes
Salt
1 bunch celery, sliced very thin
3 medium-to-large red onions, sliced thin and separated into rings
1 pound bacon, fried crisp and crumbled

2 bunches fresh parsley, finely chopped
3 cups mayonnaise
4 tablespoons white or cider vinegar
2 tablespoons granulated sugar
Salt and pepper to taste

Cook unpeeled potatoes until tender; slice as thin as possible without causing them to crumble. Place layer of sliced potatoes in very large bowl and sprinkle with salt. Top potatoes with layer of celery, then onions, then bacon, then parsley.

Combine mayonnaise, vinegar, sugar, salt and pepper. Spread several tablespoons of dressing mixture over parsley layer. Repeat layers several times, until all ingredients are used. Toss salad very gently, trying not to break up potato slices more than necessary. Chill, covered, until serving time.

Orange-Tuna-Macaroni Salad

Kathleen Kelly

*Wichita Eagle-Beacon,*Wichita, KS

Makes 6 to 8 servings

1/2 cup mayonnaise
1 teaspoon prepared mustard
1/4 teaspoon salt
1/8 teaspoon black pepper
2 large oranges, peeled and cut into bite-size pieces

1 can (7 ounces) tuna, drained and flaked
2 cups cooked and drained macaroni, cooled
1/2 cup diced celery
1/4 cup finely chopped onion

Blend mayonnaise, mustard, salt and pepper; mix with orange pieces, tuna, macaroni, celery and onion lightly but thoroughly.

Note: This salad can be made ahead and refrigerated overnight.

Broccoli Salad

Christine Arpe Gang

The Commercial Appeal, Memphis, TN

I have served this to people who usually don't like broccoli and they've loved it.

Makes 6 to 8 servings

2 bunches (2 pounds) fresh broccoli, cut into flowerets
1 cup mayonnaise
Juice of 1/2 lemon
1/2 teaspoon anchovy paste or to taste

1 small red onion, sliced thin
1 pound fresh mushrooms, sliced
Freshly ground pepper to taste

Cook broccoli in boiling water about 3 minutes and then plunge into cold water. Mix mayonnaise with lemon juice and anchovy paste. Mix drained broccoli flowerets, sliced onions (separated into rings) and mushrooms. Toss with mayonnaise mixture. Add pepper to taste.

If made in advance, let broccoli marinate in mayonnaise mixture in refrigerator, but wait until just before serving to add mushrooms and onions.

Note: Variations include using a little fresh raw spinach in addition to broccoli and adding sliced water chestnuts.

Carrot Salad

Lorrie Guttman
Tallahassee Democrat, Tallahassee, FL

Makes 8 to 12 servings

1 pound carrots, peeled and
  sliced
1 can (16 ounces) tomato sauce
1 cup granulated sugar
1/2 cup vegetable oil
3/4 cup wine vinegar
Salt and pepper to taste
1 teaspoon dry mustard
1 teaspoon (or more)
  Worcestershire sauce

Dash hot pepper sauce
  (optional)
1 medium onion, chopped
1 medium green pepper,
  chopped
1 can (16 ounces) whole
  kernel corn, drained
1/2 cup chopped celery

Boil carrots in salted water just until tender; drain and place in 2-quart covered casserole. Combine tomato sauce, sugar, oil, vinegar, salt, pepper, mustard, Worcestershire and hot pepper sauce; mix well. Pour over carrots; add onion, green pepper, corn and celery. Cover and marinate overnight.

Note: This salad will keep in the refrigerator at least 1 week.

Chinese Asparagus Salad

Pat Hanna Kuehl
Rocky Mountain News, Denver, CO

The nicest thing about spring is all the marvelous fresh asparagus. This is one of my favorite asparagus recipes.

Makes 6 to 8 servings

2 pounds fresh asparagus
1/4 cup soy sauce
1/2 teaspoon granulated sugar

1/2 teaspoon cider vinegar
1/2 teaspoon salt
2 teaspoons sesame oil

Wash and peel the asparagus with potato peeler. Cut spears diagonally in 1-1/2-inch lengths. Cook asparagus pieces in boiling water for 1 minute; drain and rinse under cold water to stop cooking.

Combine soy sauce, sugar, vinegar, salt, and oil in large bowl. Add asparagus and toss. Chill well before serving.

Chrysanthemum Salad

Bernie O'Brien

Hollywood Sun-Tattler, Hollywood, FL

*This is one for those who like to smell their flowers
and eat them, too.*

Makes 6 servings

3 large chrysanthemums,
2 yellow and 1 mauve
1/2 cup white wine vinegar
1 teaspoon honey
1 teaspoon fresh, chopped
tarragon or 1/2 teaspoon dried
Juice of 1 lemon

1/2 pound lettuce, broken into
bite-size bits
1 bunch watercress, coarsely
chopped
4 large pimiento-stuffed olives,
sliced
1/2 cup olive oil
Salt and pepper to taste

Pull petals from flowers. Combine vinegar with honey, tarragon and lemon juice in small bowl. Marinate petals in mixture for 30 minutes. Drain petals and reserve marinade. Mix petals with lettuce, watercress and olives in large bowl.

Mix olive oil with 3 tablespoons of reserved marinade; add salt and pepper. Toss salad with dressing just before serving.

IMPORTANT: Check to see if the flowers have been sprayed with anything harmful before buying them.

Continental Cauliflower Salad

Barbara McQuade
Vancouver Sun, Vancouver, British Columbia, Canada

I prefer salads that can be made ahead. This one is a great hit with guests because it's such a nice change from the usual tossed salad. I sometimes use red pepper and skip the pimiento.

Makes 8 servings

4 cups thinly sliced cauliflower
1/2 cup coarsely chopped ripe pitted olives
1 green pepper, seeded and chopped
1 can (3-1/4 ounces) chopped pimiento

1/2 cup chopped onion
1/2 cup vegetable oil
3 tablespoons lemon juice
3 tablespoons red wine vinegar
1 teaspoon salt
1/2 teaspoon granulated sugar
1/4 teaspoon pepper

Combine cauliflower, olives, green pepper, pimiento and onion in large salad bowl. Combine oil, lemon juice, vinegar, salt, sugar and pepper in small bowl; mix well. Pour dressing over vegetables. Toss to combine. Cover and refrigerate 4 hours, or overnight.

Hearts of Palm, Endive and Avocado with Caper Vinaigrette

Elaine Corn

The Courier-Journal, Louisville, KY

Makes 2 servings

1 cup drained hearts of palm   6 large leaves endive

1 ripe avocado

Caper Vinaigrette

2 tablespoons good wine vinegar 6 tablespoons fruity olive oil

1/2 teaspoon coarse salt   1 teaspoon drained capers

Few grinds black pepper

Coarsely dice hearts of palm. Peel, halve, quarter and slice avocado. Combine with hearts of palm. Line two plates with endive leaves. Divide mixture in 2 even portions and form mound in center of each salad plate.

Caper Vinaigrette: As if scrambling eggs, mix vinegar, salt, pepper and olive oil in small bowl. After blending well, stir in capers.

Spoon Caper Vinaigrette sparsely over mounded salad.

Molded Gazpacho Salad

Christine Arpe Gang
The Commercial Appeal, Memphis, TN

*When I entertain with a buffet, I like to include this
molded gazpacho salad because it is easier to serve
then soup course.*

Makes 8 to 10 servings

2 envelopes unflavored gelatin
1 can (18 ounces) tomato juice
1/2 cup lemon juice
1/2 teaspoon hot pepper sauce
2 small cloves garlic, minced
1 medium onion, grated
1/2 teaspoon salt

1 large green pepper, finely
  chopped
1 large cucumber, peeled,
  seeded and finely chopped
2 medium tomatoes, peeled and
  chopped

Sprinkle gelatin over tomato juice in small saucepan and let stand
for 5 minutes to soften. Place over low heat and stir constantly until
gelatin is dissolved. Cool.

Combine lemon juice, hot pepper sauce, garlic, onion and salt in
mixing bowl. Add tomato-gelatin mixture and mix well. Chill until
slightly thickened, stirring occasionally.

Stir in green pepper, cucumber and tomato. Turn into lightly oiled
6-cup mold and chill until set.

Mrs. Poole's Fresh Cauliflower Salad

Susan Manlin Katzman
Free-lance writer, St. Louis, MO

While in his teens, my brother often ate at the home of a friend named Pebble Poole. My brother would return raving about Mrs. Poole's pie or Mrs. Poole's stew or Mrs. Poole's bread. Everything Mrs. Poole made, according to my brother, was "sheer heaven." In fact, I heard so much about Mrs. Poole's luscious food that I called her and asked if she would share some of her recipes. She was generous, and now, like my brother, I think everything Mrs. Poole made must have been "sheer heaven." The following is her recipe. I have never met Mrs. Poole but I am deeply in her debt and would like to take this space to say, "Thank you, Mrs. Poole, for years and years of pleasure."

Makes 6 servings

1 cup fine dry bread crumbs
3 tablespoons butter
13 ounces romaine lettuce
(9 to 10 cups bite-size pieces)
1 cup mayonnaise

2 tablespoons grated Parmesan cheese
1 tablespoon fresh lemon juice
1 small clove garlic, mashed
Salt and pepper to taste
1/2 head of cauliflower

Brown bread crumbs in butter and set aside to cool. Break lettuce into bite-size pieces and put into a pretty salad bowl. Combine mayonnaise, Parmesan cheese, lemon juice and garlic. Season with salt and pepper. Pour mixture over lettuce and toss well. Top with bread crumbs; don't toss. Grate cauliflower and sprinkle over bread crumbs. Serve immediately without tossing.

Mustard Ring

Nancy Millard
Muncie Star, Muncie, IN

*I knew Dorothy Doss in Dallas, Texas. Although she
said she didn't like to cook, her buffets always were
marvelous. My favorite memory is of a piquant mustard
ring, which she served with baked ham.*

Makes 12 servings

4 eggs
3/4 cup granulated sugar
2 tablespoons dry mustard
1 package (1 tablespoon)
   unflavored gelatin

1 tablespoon water
1/2 cup white vinegar
1/2 cup water
Dash salt
1 cup heavy cream, whipped

Beat eggs well. Combine sugar and dry mustard; beat into eggs.
Soften gelatin in 1 tablespoon water and dissolve over low heat; add
to egg mixture with vinegar and 1/2 cup water. Add salt.

Cook mixture in top of double boiler over simmering, not boiling,
water, stirring constantly, until thickened. Cool by stirring over pan of
cold water.

When mixture is cool, fold in whipped cream. Spoon mixture into
oiled 1-1/2-quart ring mold. Chill until firm.

Note: For a more piquant flavor, use 1 cup white vinegar in place
of 1/2 cup vinegar and 1/2 cup water.

Nana's Cucumbers

Janice Okun
Buffalo News, Buffalo, NY

This is an old family recipe, similar to, but not exactly like, many other cucumber salad recipes. The difference lies in the onion rings and copious amounts of freshly ground black pepper.

Makes 4 to 6 servings

3 cucumbers
1 medium white onion
White vinegar

Salt and sugar to taste
Freshly ground black pepper

Slice cucumbers paper thin (peeling or not as you wish). Slice onion into rings.

Place cucumber in clean dish towel; roll towel and squeeze—hard. Try to remove as much moisture from cucumbers as you can.

Place squeezed cucumbers in bowl; add onion rings. Cover with vinegar to which small amount of cold water and hint of sugar have been added. Add salt. Sprinkle freely with pepper.

Refrigerate and let stand several hours—the colder the better.

Note: This makes a wonderful accompaniment for cold meats.

Oriental Shrimp Salad

Karen K. Marshall

St. Louis Globe-Democrat, St. Louis, MO

This recipe is an adaption of the top winner several years ago in the Globe-Democrat's *recipe contest.*

Makes 3 servings

2 cups peeled and cooked shrimp

1 cup bean sprouts, rinsed and drained

1 can (8 ounces) water chestnuts, drained and finely chopped

1/4 cup finely chopped green onions

1/4 cup finely chopped celery

1 cup chow mein noodles

Soy Mayonnaise

3/4 cup mayonnaise

1 tablespoon lemon juice

1 tablespoon soy sauce

1/4 teaspoon ground ginger

If shrimp are large, cut into halves or thirds. Combine shrimp, bean sprouts, water chestnuts, green onions and celery in medium-size bowl.

Combine Soy Mayonnaise ingredients thoroughly; add to shrimp mixture and toss to mix well.

Refrigerate, covered, until serving time. Just before serving add chow mein noodles and mix well.

Note: This recipe can also be made with cooked, chopped chicken.

Peanut Crunch Salad

Beverly Daniel
The Bellingham Herald, Bellingham, WA

*One of my closest friends gave this recipe to me
because she knows my strong liking for peanuts. It's a
good accompaniment for charcoal-cooked steaks or
baked ham.*

Makes 6 to 8 servings

4 cups shredded cabbage
1 cup finely chopped celery
1/2 cup sour cream
1/2 cup mayonnaise
1 teaspoon salt
1/4 cup chopped green onion
1/4 cup chopped green pepper

1/2 cup chopped cucumber
1 tablespoon butter
1/2 cup coarsely chopped dry
    roasted peanuts
2 tablespoons grated Parmesan
    cheese

Toss cabbage and celery together. Chill. Combine sour cream, mayonnaise, salt, onion, green pepper and cucumber in small bowl. Chill.

Just before serving, melt butter in small skillet. Add peanuts and heat until lightly browned. Immediately stir in cheese. Toss chilled vegetables with dressing. Sprinkle peanut mixture on top and serve.

The Original Caesar Salad

Bernie O'Brien
Hollywood Sun-Tattler, Hollywood, FL

In the spring of 1965, the following story was sent to me — before I was food editor of the Hollywood Sun-Tattler — by Rosa Cardini of Los Angeles, who is a daughter of Caesar:
In 1924, over a holiday weekend Caesar's Place—a restaurant in Tijuana, Mexico — ran short of food. Caesar experimented, and that evening the first Caesar Salad was served. While the waiters kibitzed, Caesar demonstrated his creation. "Take everything to each table," he instructed, "and make a ceremony of fixing the salad. Plenty of fanfare. Let guests think they're having the specialty of the house." And the guests did.
You'll find many variations of Caesar Salad, but here Rosa Cardlini shares her father's authentic recipe and salad know-how.

Makes 6 large servings

Garlic-flavored Olive Oil
1 cup olive oil or salad oil   6 cloves garlic
(or 1/2 cup of each)

Caesar Croutons
1 cup bread cubes (approx.)   Grated Parmesan cheese

Salad
3 medium heads romaine,   Salt
  chilled, dry and crisp   Dash Worcestershire sauce
2 to 3 tablespoons wine vinegar 5 or 6 tablespoons grated
Juice of 1 lemon   Parmesan cheese
1 or 2 one-minute coddled eggs (Anchovies for garnish,
Freshly ground pepper   optional)

Garlic-flavored olive oil: Prepare one to several days early. Slice cloves of garlic lengthwise in quarters and let stand in olive oil.

Caesar croutons: Preheat oven to 225°F. Cut bread in strips one way, then across 5 times, to make cubes. Spread out on cookie sheet; pour small amount garlic-flavored oil over cubes. Heat in oven for 2 hours. Sprinkle croutons with grated Parmesan cheese. Store in jar and refrigerate to keep crispness.

Romaine: Wash 24 hours ahead if possible. Pat leaves dry with towel; wrap in fresh towels and refrigerate.

To prepare salad: Break romaine leaves in 2- to 3-inch widths. At last minute before serving, place romaine in chilled salad bowl. Drizzle about 1/3 cup garlic-flavored oil over greens, then vinegar, then lemon juice. Break in eggs. Grind flurry of pepper over all. Season with salt and dash Worcestershire. Sprinkle with cheese. Roll-toss (see Caesar Salad Helps below) 6 or 7 times, or until dressing is throughly combined and every leaf is coated. Add croutons; toss 1 or 2 times. Serve at once on chilled dinner plates.

Garnish with rolled anchovies, if desired.

Note: The anchovies, now a familiar ingredient in Caesar Salad, didn't become part of the recipe until some 10 years later.

Caesar Salad Helps

Croutons: Slow toasting of bread insures that croutons will stay crunchy when tossed with greens and dressing. Cubes should be so dry they'd float on water.

Romaine: Wrapping washed and dried leaves in towels and refrigerating helps them to retain their crispness. Always break or tear leaves, never cut, or they may take on an unattractive brown edge. This method may be used for any salad greens.

Dressing the greens: For even distribution, always follow a Z-line as you pour oil, vinegar and lemon juice over salad. Always add oil first to coat leaves—salad stays crisper that way.

Roll-toss to mix: With salad spoon in right hand, fork in left, go down to bottom of bowl with one tool while going up and over with other. "Roll" salad until every leaf shines with dressing.

Serving art: Start with chilled bowl and chilled plates. Traditionally, Caesar Salad is served on dinner-size plates, whether for the main course at lunch, or in smaller helpings for an appetizer. Don't overlook the drama of handsome accessories—the giant bowl, spoon and fork for tossing, little bowls to hold ingredients, oil and vinegar cruets, tall pepper mill and salt shaker.

Southwest Salad

Jane Baker
The Phoenix Gazette, Phoenix, AZ

This is an unusual approach to ordinary macaroni salad. I often take it to potluck suppers. You can substitute almost any vegetables you like. Best of all, it can be made several days in advance.

Makes 10 to 12 servings

1 pound small shell macaroni, cooked al dente and drained
3/4 cup red wine vinegar
1/4 cup vegetable oil
1 cup sliced celery
1/2 cup chopped green pepper
6 green onions, sliced (with green tops)
1/4 teaspoon Worcestershire sauce
Several dashes hot pepper sauce
2 to 3 tablespoons chopped green chilies
Salt and pepper to taste
1 can (16 ounces) garbanzo beans, drained
1 can (12 ounces) corn, drained
1/2 cup chopped black olives
1/3 cup mayonnaise (approx.)

Put cooked macaroni in large salad bowl. Pour vinegar over macaroni and let stand while preparing other ingredients. Add oil, celery, green pepper, onions, Worcestershire, hot pepper sauce, chilies, salt, pepper, beans, corn, olives and mayonnaise to macaroni mixture; mix well.

Cover and refrigerate for 2 to 3 days. Taste for seasonings before serving. (There should be a suggestion of the chilies and the tart tang of vinegar, but only a minimal amount of mayonnaise.)

Tangy Cole Slaw

Helen Dollaghan

The Denver Post, Denver, CO

Makes 8 servings

1-1/2 cups mayonnaise (Do not use salad dressing)
3 tablespoons bottled sandwich spread
3/4 teaspoon dry mustard
2 tablespoons dried parsley flakes

1 medium head cabbage, shredded
3/4 cup drained sweet pickle relish
1/2 cup chopped celery
3/4 cup chopped onion
Paprika

Combine mayonnaise, sandwich spread, mustard and parsley. Mix well; set aside. Toss cabbage with relish, celery and onion. Add enough mayonnaise mixture to moisten all ingredients. Mix lightly but thoroughly. Sprinkle with paprika.

Note: Dressing can be stored tightly covered, in refrigerator, for a week or longer. Makes approximately 1-1/2 cups.

Zippy Zucchini Salad

Mary Scourtes
The Tampa Tribune, Tampa, FL

This recipe was created when I started to cook zucchini one night; then my plans changed and I went out to dinner. The zucchini was tossed into the refrigerator. The next night, I took it out and served it on salad greens instead of reheating it.

Makes 4 to 6 servings

1 clove garlic
2 teaspoons olive oil
3 zucchini, sliced into 1/4-inch rounds
1 teaspoon granulated sugar
1/2 cup black olives, sliced
1/4 cup slivered almonds
3 tablespoons cider vinegar
1/3 cup chili sauce

1/3 cup bottled spicy, sweet French salad dressing
2 tablespoons minced fresh parsley
1/2 teaspoon dried tarragon
1/4 teaspoon dried oregano
Salt and pepper to taste
Salad greens

Sauté garlic in olive oil. Add zucchini and stir-fry until just tender. Discard garlic. Remove zucchini from pan and place in bowl or other container. Add sugar to pan, then add olives, almonds, vinegar, chili sauce, salad dressing, parsley, tarragon, oregano, salt and pepper. Cook over moderate heat about 2 minutes to blend flavors. Pour sauce over zucchini; cover and chill several hours or overnight. Serve on salad greens.

Main Courses

Lake George Shrimp

Kingsley Belle
The Chronicle, Glens Falls, NY

A veterinarian who fishes as a hobby introduced me to this interesting recipe. It makes use of perch, a common fish in the lakes and ponds east of the Rockies. It's called Lake George Shrimp because, after being cooked, the perch resembles the seafaring crustacean both in taste and appearance.

Makes 4 to 6 servings

2 dozen perch fillets, cut in
  1/2 x 3-inch strips
4 quarts boiling water

1/4 cup salt
Ice water
Cocktail sauce

Put perch strips into sieve or colander and immerse in boiling water to which salt has been added. Allow strips to boil about 3 minutes, or until they become white and flaky and curl up.

Lift fish-filled sieve out of water and place immediately in an ice water bath. Leave until fish has cooled.

Arrange cooled fish pieces on platter and serve with cocktail sauce.

Note: The fish also is good served warm, with tartar sauce. When warm, it tastes remarkably like lobster.

Bass, pike, pickerel or blue gill can be used in place of perch.

The large amount of salt is necessary to give shrimp-like flavor.

German-Style Venison Roast

Barbara Gibbs Ostmann
St. Louis Post-Dispatch, St. Louis, MO

My husband is a hunter. He hunts everything — deer, wild turkey, rabbits, ducks, squirrel, elk, bear, antelope, quail. And everything he hunts, we eat. When my family comes to visit, they always examine the main course suspiciously and ask if it is something weird. I've converted even the most die-hard venison-haters with this recipe. They always ask for seconds. A German couple shared this recipe with me.

Makes 4 to 8 servings

1 roast of venison
   (4 to 5 pounds)
6 strips bacon
3/4 cup butter
Salt and pepper to taste

1 cup hot water
1/2 cup sour cream
1/2 cup all-purpose flour
1/2 cup half-and-half or light
   cream

Lard well-trimmed roast with bacon strips. Melt butter in skillet. Brown meat lightly on all sides. Sprinkle generously with salt and pepper. Place meat in roasting pan along with melted butter. (Layer the bacon over the roast at this point instead of larding it, if you prefer.) Rinse skillet with 1 cup hot water and pour over meat. Cover and bake in 350°F. oven 2 to 2-1/2 hours. Baste with juices several times during cooking. About 30 minutes before it is done, remove roast from oven and make gravy.

Gravy: Combine sour cream, flour and half-and-half; stir until smooth. Pour mixture into meat juices in pan. (It may be necessary to remove meat in order to stir mixture into juices; return meat to pan.)

Return pan to oven, reduce oven heat to 325°F. and continue baking for last 30 minutes of cooking time, basting roast with gravy occasionally.

Note: I often use a clay cooker for the roasting pan; I think it is even better in the clay cooker.

I like to serve this with boiled potatoes, red cabbage and cranberry relish.

Maggie Steffen's Turkey Pot Pie

Susan Manlin Katzman
Free-lance writer, St. Louis, MO

I remember with special delight the Christmas food at my grandmother's farm. Granny was a wonderful cook who believed everything she served during the holidays should be like Christmas itself, rich and sumptuous. By Christmas Eve, when we arrived for our family reunion, her house bulged with holiday treats. For me, though, the best dishes came at noon on Christmas Day, after the presents and before the journey home. We would sit in the parlor around a fire and feast on hot, yeasty pan rolls, ice-cold cranberry relish and succulent turkey pot pie freshly made from Christmas Eve's turkey. The pie bubbled with chunks of sweet home-grown vegetables and generous mouthfuls of tender turkey. I found this recipe while sorting through Granny's "holiday box", and I offer it in tribute to a lovely woman and an extraordinary cook.

Makes 6 servings

5-1/4 cups chicken broth
3 carrots, pared and cut into
  l-inch pieces
1 small onion, diced
1/4 pound fresh mushrooms,
  sliced

2/3 cup frozen peas, thawed
3/4 cup butter
2/3 cup all-purpose flour
Salt and pepper to taste
4 cups cooked turkey, cut into
  large, bite-size pieces

Crust
1 cup all-purpose flour
1/2 teaspoon salt
7 tablespoons solid shortening

3 tablespoons ice water
1 egg yolk
1 tablespoon light cream or
  milk

Bring chicken broth to boil in large saucepan. Add carrots and onion and cook until almost tender. Add mushrooms and peas, cook 5 minutes. Remove vegetables from broth. Reserve vegetables. Strain broth and set 4 cups aside.

Melt butter and whisk in flour. Cook, stirring constantly, 2 minutes. Gradually whisk in reserved hot chicken broth. Cook until mixture thickens and bubbles 1 minute. Season to taste with salt and pepper.

Spoon 1/4-inch layer of sauce into bottom of 2-quart baking dish. Place same amount of sauce in small bowl and set aside. Mix turkey, vegetables and remaining sauce. Put turkey mixture in baking dish and cover with reserved sauce. Refrigerate until cool.

Crust: Mix flour and salt. Add shortening and mix lightly with fingertips to form coarse crumbs. Add water, 1 tablespoon at a time, and mix with fork until pastry is moist enough to hold together. Knead on lightly floured surface until dough is smooth, about 20 strokes. Wrap in wax paper and chill 1 hour.

Preheat oven to 400°F. Roll pie crust dough about 1/4-inch thick. Cut dough to fit top of baking dish, allowing for 1-inch overhang. Fit dough over turkey filling, tucking edges under. Press dough against side of dish with fork to seal. Cut 1-1/2-inch circle from center of dough as steam vent. If you like, decorate top of pie with excess dough. (Stick decorations on dough with water.) Combine egg yolk and cream; brush top of pie. Bake in oven 40 minutes, or until crust is brown and filling is bubbly.

Chicken Casserole

Ellen Carlson

St. Paul Dispatch and Pioneer Press, St. Paul, MN

This is an old favorite that I have made often because it serves eight generously.

Makes 8 servings

3/4 cup chopped celery
1 to 2 tablespoons chopped onion
1 tablespoon chopped green pepper
2 tablespoons butter or margarine
2 cups soft bread crumbs

4 cups diced cooked chicken
1 cup cooked rice
2 tablespoons chopped pimiento
1 teaspoon salt
4 eggs
1-1/2 cups milk
1-1/2 cups chicken broth

Mushroom Sauce

6 tablespoons all-purpose flour
1/4 cup melted butter
2 cups chicken broth
1 can (4 ounces) sliced mushrooms, drained
1 teaspoon chopped fresh parsley

1 teaspoon salt
1/2 teaspoon paprika
1 teaspoon lemon juice
1 cup light cream or half-and-half

Sauté celery, onion and green pepper in butter. Combine sautéed vegetables with bread crumbs, chicken, rice, pimiento and salt in large mixing bowl. Beat eggs in medium-size bowl, then add milk and broth. Stir liquid mixture into chicken mixture. Spread in lightly greased 13x9x2-inch baking dish. Bake in 350°F. oven 50 to 60 minutes. To serve, cut into squares and top with mushroom sauce.

Mushroom Sauce: Stir flour into melted butter in skillet. Slowly add chicken broth; stir over low heat until mixture thickens. Stir in mushrooms, parsley, salt, paprika, lemon juice and cream. Gently stir mixture over low heat until hot.

Spoon sauce over portions of Chicken Casserole.

Cheese in a Chicken Pocket

Evelyn Wavpotich
Island Packet, Hilton Head Island, SC

Chicken is a favorite at our house partly, because it lends itself so well to experimentation. My husband came up with this delicious rendition.

Makes 4 servings

2 whole chicken breasts, split and boned with skin left on
1/2 cup diced Mozzarella cheese
1/3 cup bread crumbs made from Italian or French bread
5 tablespoons unsalted butter
4 teaspoons diced cooked ham

Cut pocket in each chicken piece and stuff generously with cheese. Tuck and shape each piece until you have a small loaf with skin on top. Wrap individually in foil and steam 20 minutes. Remove foil and discard skin from chicken.

Toast bread crumbs until golden in 2 tablespoons melted butter; set aside. Heat ham in remaining butter. Dress chicken with bread crumbs and ham. Serve immediately.

Brunch Soufflé

Mary Alice Powell

The Blade, Toledo, OH

This recipe finds its way to many a brunch party in northwestern Ohio because it not only can, but must, be made the night before.

Makes 8 servings

1 pound mild pork sausage
6 eggs
2 cups milk
1 teaspoon salt, or to taste

1 tablespoon dry mustard
6 slices white bread, cubed
  (crusts removed, if desired)
1 cup grated Cheddar cheese

Brown sausage; drain and cool. Crumble sausage into bowl. Beat eggs in another bowl and add milk, salt, mustard and bread cubes; mix well. Add cheese and sausage; mix again. Spoon into 12x8x2-inch glass baking dish. Cover and refrigerate overnight.

Remove dish from refrigerator. Bake in 350°F. oven 45 minutes, or until egg mixture is set. Cut into squares to serve.

Broiled Shrimp with Rosemary

Anne Byrn Phillips

The Atlanta Journal-Constitution, Atlanta, GA

Makes 2 servings (or 4 to 6 appetizers)

1 cup olive oil
6 cloves garlic, minced
1 tablespoon dried rosemary or
  2 tablespoons fresh rosemary
1/4 teaspoon cayenne
1/4 cup finely minced fresh
  parsley

1 cup fresh lemon juice
1 tablespoon freshly grated
  lemon rind
1 dozen raw jumbo shrimp,
  shelled and deveined
  (10 to 15 per pound)

Mix oil, garlic, rosemary, cayenne, parsley, lemon juice and rind in non-metallic bowl. Add shrimp. Cover and refrigerate 4 to 24 hours. Stir occasionally.

Remove shrimp from marinade. Broil as close to heat source as possible about 4 minutes per side. Baste shrimp with marinade once during cooking. Serve at once, or refrigerate and serve cold.

Broiled Sea Bass with Fennel Butter

Donna Lee
The Providence Journal and Bulletin, Providence, RI

Makes 4 servings

1/4 cup butter, melted
3 tablespoons chopped fresh
  fennel or 2 tablespoons fennel
  seeds, crushed
1/4 teaspoon salt
1 tablespoon fresh lemon juice

Freshly ground pepper
1 sea bass or other fish
  (2 to 2-1/2 pounds), cleaned
  and ready to cook
Parsley and lemon for garnish

Combine butter with fennel, salt, lemon juice and freshly ground pepper. Rinse fish and pat dry. Brush inside and out with fennel butter. (Some will be left for basting.)

Place on oiled broiler rack. Broil 8 to 10 minutes on each side, about 5 inches from heat. Baste several times with fennel butter. Garnish with parsley and lemon.

Note: If you have fresh fennel, you may also put several whole sprigs of washed fennel into the cavity of the fish. Fresh dill weed may be substituted for fennel.

Rice pilaf is an excellent accompaniment.

Beef Steak and Kidney Pie

Elizabeth Sparks

Winston-Salem Journal, Winston-Salem, NC

Beef Steak and Kidney Pie may not be everyone's cup of tea, but I think it is the best thing I have ever put in my mouth. The origin of the recipe is unusual. When a meeting of the International Wine and Food Society was held in England a few years ago, the group went from London to Torquay. On the return trip, lunch was served aboard the train. A waiter came out of the kitchen carrying a pie. He stopped at the first table and spooned an opening into the top of the pie. Fragrant steam literally poured out. Members of the society, who had been feasting for days, almost swooned over the goodness of the pie. When I returned to the States, I wrote for the recipe, never expecting to get it. It came. I tried it on a rainy Sunday afternoon, and it was every bit as good as that one on the train.

Makes 8 servings

3/4 pound calf kidney (or beef liver)
Salted water
2 tablespoons all-purpose flour
1 teaspoon salt
3/4 teaspoon freshly ground black pepper
2 pounds beef steak, cut into bite-size pieces
4 tablespoons butter
4 shallots, finely chopped
1 cup beef bouillon
1 bay leaf
1 teaspoon chopped fresh parsley
Pinch ground cloves
Pinch marjoram, crushed
1/2 pound fresh mushrooms, sliced and sautéed
1 tablespoon Worcestershire sauce
Pastry for 10-inch top crust

Clean and split kidney; remove fat and large tubes. Soak in salted water 1 hour. Dry and cut into 1/4-inch slices. Mix flour, salt and pepper; roll kidney and beef pieces in flour mixture. Melt butter in heavy pot and sauté shallots. When shallots have taken on a little color, add beef and kidney; brown lightly, turning. Add bouillon, bay leaf, parsley, cloves and marjoram. Stir; cover and simmer 1 to 1-1/4 hours, or until meat is tender. Add mushrooms, and Worcestershire. If liquid is too thin, thicken with smooth paste of flour and water.

Grease deep 10-inch baking dish. Place pie funnel in center. Add meat mixture and allow to cool in refrigerator.

Meanwhile, prepare pastry. Place pastry over meat, sealing pastry edges to edge of dish. Make vents in pastry to allow steam to escape. Bake in 450°F. oven 8 to 10 minutes; lower heat to 375° and continue baking 15 minutes, or until crust is golden.

Baked Chicken Breasts with Gruyère and Mushrooms

Pat Hanna Kuehl
Rocky Mountain News, Denver, CO

The first "company dish" I learned when I moved into my first apartment is still a favorite. It can be made ahead, then warmed to serving temperature. I serve this recipe with rice pilaf, fresh asparagus with lemon butter, and a green salad with a spiced peach half for garnish.

Makes 4 servings

2 to 3 chicken breasts, boned and skinned
4 eggs, well beaten
1/2 teaspoon salt
1 cup fine bread crumbs
8 tablespoons butter

1/2 pound fresh mushrooms, sliced
4 ounces Gruyère cheese, shredded
1 cup chicken stock
Juice of 1 lemon

Cut boned breasts into strips. Marinate in egg and salt mixture for 1 hour. Roll chicken in bread crumbs to coat. Brown lightly in butter in small pan. Transfer to 1-1/2-quart casserole. Slice mushrooms over chicken. Sprinkle cheese over mushrooms. Pour chicken stock over all. Bake in 350°F. oven 30 minutes or until heated through. Pour fresh lemon juice over casserole just before serving.

Sweet-Sour Pineapple Chicken

Natalie Haughton
Daily News, Van Nuys, CA

Sweet -sour recipes of all sorts rank high in popularity with readers. This is one of my favorites, and it goes together in a breeze. It makes a good company offering, too, with plenty of hot rice.

Makes approximately 4 servings

2 whole chicken breasts or
4 chicken breast halves
(approx. 1-3/4 pounds)
1 large onion, cut in thin
wedges
1 green pepper, Cut in 3/4-inch
squares
4 tablespoons vegetable oil,
divided

2 tablespoons vinegar
1 tablespoon cornstarch
1 can (20 ounces) pineapple
chunks in juice
2 tablespoons ketchup
2 tablespoons light brown sugar
1 large tomato, cut in eighths
Salt or soy sauce to taste
Hot cooked rice

Skin and bone chicken breasts. With sharp knife, cut chicken into l-inch squares. Sauté onion and green pepper in 2 tablespoons hot oil in large skillet, stirring until vegetables are crisp-tender; remove to dish and set aside.

In same skillet, heat remaining 2 tablespoons oil until hot. Add chicken pieces and stir-fry over high heat until chicken cooks through and turns white, 5 to 7 minutes.

Mix vinegar and cornstarch; combine with juice drained from pineapple, ketchup and brown sugar. Stir into chicken in skillet. Cook, stirring constantly, until sauce clears, boils and thickens. Return onions and green pepper to skillet. Add pineapple chunks. Cover and cook a few more minutes, until heated through. Stir in tomato. Season with salt or soy sauce to taste.

Serve over hot cooked rice.

Broiled Fish Fillets Amandine

Marilyn McDevitt Rubin
The Pittsburgh Press, Pittsburgh, PA

Makes 4 to 6 servings

1-1/2 to 2 pounds fish fillets
(any mild-flavored fish)
1/4 cup quick-mixing flour

2 teaspoons paprika
1-1/2 teaspoons salt
1 to 2 tablespoons vegetable oil

Lemon-Butter Sauce
3 tablespoons butter or
margarine

2 teaspoons lemon juice
3 or 4 drops hot pepper sauce

Toasted Slivered Almonds
2 tablespoons butter per serving

1 tablespoon slivered almonds
per serving

Rinse fish fillets and pat dry with paper towel. Combine flour, paprika and salt; mix thoroughly. Coat fillets with flour mixture. Lightly oil shallow baking pan or casserole. Arrange flour-coated fillets in bottom of pan in one layer.

Lemon-Butter Sauce: Melt butter, lemon juice and hot pepper sauce in small pan.

Brush fillets with sauce. Broil fish 4 to 5 inches from source of heat, basting occasionally with additional sauce, until slight crust forms on surface, or until fish becomes opaque and flesh flakes easily when tested with fork. While fillets are broiling, prepare Toasted Almonds.

Toasted Almonds: Melt butter in small skillet over medium-high heat. When foaming subsides, add slivered almonds. Toss nuts in hot fat with fork until nuts and butter are golden brown, watching carefully that they do not burn. Lift nuts from fat with slotted spoon and drain on paper towel to crisp. Reserve butter and keep hot.

Pour hot butter over fillets when done and sprinkle with toasted almonds.

Note: Do not overcook fish, and do not turn fillets while broiling unless they are very thick.

Flounder, sole, turbot, red snapper, mackerel, bluefish and white-fish are among my choices for this dish.

Smelts Baked in Orange Sauce

Claire Barriger
Free-lance writer, Ottawa, Ontario, Canada

Smelts are small, slender, silvery fish with a transparent olive-green coloration along their backs. They rarely grow longer than ten inches. But what they lack in size, they more than make up for in flavor.

Makes 6 to 8 servings

2 pounds smelts, thawed and
  dressed
Salt and pepper to taste

1/4 cup butter or margarine,
  melted
1/4 cup orange juice
1 teaspoon grated orange rind

Arrange smelts in greased baking dish. Sprinkle with salt and pepper. Combine melted butter with orange juice and rind. Pour over fish. Bake in 450°F. oven 10 minutes.

Note: Smelts are inexpensive and can be cooked in the same ways as other fish — breaded and fried in butter, dipped in batter and deep-fried or cooked in a sauce with vegetables.

Baked Boston Bluefish

Phyllis Hanes
The Christian Science Monitor

Makes 6 servings

6 bluefish fillets
Salt and pepper to taste
1 teaspoon dried tarragon
1 teaspoon dried thyme

1 teaspoon dried oregano
1-1/2 teaspoons chopped fresh
  parsley
Olive oil

Sprinkle fish with salt and pepper to taste and place in baking dish. Combine tarragon, thyme, oregano and parsley; sprinkle over fish. Sprinkle all with olive oil. Bake in 350°F. oven 20 minutes or until fish flakes easily with fork.

Sweet-Sour Pot Roast

Charlotte Hansen
The Jamestown Sun, Jamestown, ND

The flavor of the meat in this recipe is extraordinarily good. It also makes delicious leftovers.

Makes 6 servings

1 tablespoon solid shortening
4 pounds chuck or rump beef roast
2 onions, sliced
1/4 teaspoon pepper

1/4 teaspoon ground cloves
1/4 cup honey
1/4 cup granulated sugar
Juice of 2 lemons
1 teaspoon salt or to taste

Heat shortening in Dutch oven or heavy skillet with tight-fitting lid. Add meat and onions; brown, turning frequently. Add pepper, cloves, honey, sugar, lemon juice and salt. Cover tightly. Simmer slowly over low heat or bake in 300°F. oven 3 to 3-1/2 hours, until meat is tender.

Trail Ride Eggs (Huevos Mexicanos)

Billie Bledsoe
San Antonio Express and News, San Antonio, TX

The spring roundup of range cattle was a tradition in Texas for nearly a hundred years. Nowadays, the annual Rodeo and Stock Show revives memories of the good old days. Early in February, groups of trail riders set out a week or so in advance and converge on San Antonio. This is a typical campfire breakfast.

Makes 2 servings

2 tablespoons butter or margarine
4 eggs, lightly beaten
Salt to taste

1 whole canned green chili, sliced
1 tomato, peeled, seeded and chopped (optional)
1/2 cup grated sharp Cheddar

Melt butter in skillet. Add eggs and scramble, making certain eggs remain moist. Add salt to taste. Add sliced green chili and toss lightly with eggs. If using tomato, add after green chili. Stir in gently just to heat through. Remove to serving plate and top with grated cheese.

Steve's Favorite Lasagna

Mary Frances Phillips
San Jose Mercury and News, San Jose, CA

Whenever I ask my son, who is twenty-one and a student at Cal Poly, San Luis Obispo, what he wants when he comes home from school, it is always the same lasagna. Now, however, he can whip it up as well as I can. He says this is better the second day.

Makes 8 servings

2 pounds lean ground beef
1 medium onion, chopped
1 clove garlic, chopped
1 can (16 ounces) tomatoes
2 cans (8 ounces each) pizza sauce
1 teaspoon salt
1/2 teaspoon dried basil, crumbled

1 teaspoon dried oregano, crumbled
1 package (8 ounces) lasagna noodles, cooked and drained
1 cup small curd cottage cheese
2 cups grated Mozzarella cheese
1/2 cup grated Parmesan cheese

Brown beef, onion and garlic in large frying pan. Separate beef into chunks; pour off drippings. Add tomatoes, pizza sauce, salt, basil and oregano. Cover and cook over low heat for 20 minutes.

Reserve 1 cup meat sauce for top of lasagna. Place 1 cup sauce in bottom of greased 13x9-inch baking dish. Top with half the noodles, cover with half the remaining meat sauce, 1/2 cup cottage cheese, 1 cup Mozzarella cheese and 1/4 cup Parmesan cheese.

Repeat with remaining noodles, meat sauce, cottage cheese and Mozzarella — no Parmesan cheese. Put reserved meat sauce over top of assembled dish. Sprinkle with remaining Parmesan cheese. Bake in 350°F. oven 30 minutes. Let stand 10 minutes to make slicing easier.

Spinach Lasagna

Eleanor Ostman
St. Paul Pioneer Press and Dispatch, St. Paul, MN

It pays to advertise. I first tasted this recipe at the annual potluck at my son's grade school. When I wrote about it in my Sunday column, a reader who had contributed it to the potluck volunteered to share its secret. This very rich and buttery lasagna, now a favorite in many Minnesota homes, is even better reheated.

Makes 8 servings

8 ounces lasagna noodles, cooked and drained
2 packages (10 ounces each) frozen chopped spinach, cooked and drained
2 pounds cottage cheese
2 eggs

1 tablespoon chopped fresh parsley or 1 teaspoon crushed dried parsley
1/2 cup butter, softened
Salt, pepper and garlic powder to taste
1 pound Monterey Jack cheese, grated
1 cup grated Parmesan cheese

Cook noodles according to package directions; drain. Cook spinach according to package directions; drain. Mix cottage cheese, eggs, parsley, butter, salt, pepper and garlic powder in bowl. Grease lasagna pan or 13x9x2-inch rectangular baking dish. Place layer of noodles in pan, followed by layers of cottage cheese mixture, Monterey Jack cheese, spinach and Parmesan cheese. Repeat layers. Bake in 350°F. oven 30 minutes.

Variation: For a less buttery version, omit butter from cottage cheese mixture. After arranging layers, drizzle with about 2 tablespoons melted butter, then bake as directed.

Saffron Mussels

Phyllis Hanes
The Christian Science Monitor

Fresh mussels are at their best when scrubbed, steamed in a small amount of water, then served in the shell with melted butter and garlic for dipping, much like steamed clams. They are also good cold, having been stuffed with a well-seasoned mixture, such as in this recipe.

Makes approximately 6 servings

1 small onion, chopped
1 leek, chopped
3 tablespoons olive oil
1 tomato, peeled and seeded
2 garlic cloves

1 sprig fresh thyme, or
   1/4 teaspoon dried thyme
   crumbled
1/2 bay leaf
1 teaspoon powdered saffron
1 cup water
36 mussels

Sauté chopped onion and leek in oil in large pot. Add tomato, garlic, thyme, bay leaf, saffron and water. Cook slowly until almost all liquid has evaporated.

Add mussels which have been scrubbed and washed. Cook until shells open, from 12 to 15 minutes. Remove and discard one half shell of each mussel. Add 1/2 teaspoon sauce to each mussel. Chill thoroughly.

Red Devil Franks

Bernie Arnold

Nashville Banner, Nashville, TN

This is an ordinary recipe, but it's great when raising a bunch of hungry kids.

Makes 8 to 10 servings

1 cup finely chopped onion
2 cloves garlic, minced
4 tablespoons margarine
1/2 teaspoon salt
1/8 teaspoon pepper
1-1/2 tablespoons prepared mustard

1-1/2 tablespoons Worcestershire sauce
1-1/2 teaspoons granulated sugar
1/2 cup chili sauce
1 pound frankfurters (8 to 10)
Frankfurter buns (8 to 10)

Cook onion and garlic in margarine over low heat until onion is tender, about 10 minutes. Stir frequently. Add salt, pepper, Worcestershire, mustard, sugar and chili sauce. Continue heating until flavors are well blended, about 5 minutes.

Split frankfurters lengthwise and arrange split-side up in shallow pan. Spoon sauce over frankfurters and heat under broiler until frankfurters are hot and sauce is bubbly, 3 to 5 minutes.

Serve hot on split, toasted frankfurter buns. Spoon on extra sauce.

Rave-Bringing Beef Ribs

Deni Hamilton

The Courier-Journal, Louisville, KY

I invented this recipe when I first noticed beef plate ribs (the steer's spare ribs) in my supermarket. They were very inexpensive and I couldn't pass them up. But there weren't any recipes for them in any of my cookbooks. Of course, beef plate ribs can be barbecued just like pork spare ribs, but I wanted something without gooey, sweet tomato sauce.

Makes 4 servings

4 to 5 pounds beef plate ribs
1 cup double-strength coffee
1 tablespoon liquid smoke

1 tablespoon light brown sugar
1 tablespoon Worcestershire sauce

Preheat oven to 350°F.

Score ribs on both sides between bones, or cut all the way through. Lay ribs in bottom of roasting pan with tight-fitting lid.

Combine coffee, liquid smoke, sugar and Worcestershire; pour over ribs. Cover and bake in oven 2 hours, or until ribs are almost tender. Remove cover and continue baking until ribs are browned and tender, another 20 minutes or so. Ribs may be turned over after 10 minutes to brown other side.

Pork Satay

Nancy Pappas
The Louisville Times, Louisville, KY

I learned how to make this Indonesian recipe from my Swiss aunt.

Makes 4 servings

2 tablespoons smooth peanut butter
2 tablespoons ground coriander
1/8 teaspoon cayenne
1/4 teaspoon freshly ground black pepper
1 clove garlic, chopped

2 tablespoons finely chopped onion
1 teaspoon salt
1 tablespoon light brown sugar
3 tablespoons lemon juice
1/4 cup soy sauce
1-1/2 pounds lean pork
Olive oil or melted butter

Mix peanut butter, coriander, cayenne, black pepper, garlic, onion, salt, sugar, lemon juice and soy sauce in bowl to make marinade. Cut pork into cubes and toss with marinade. Cover bowl with plastic wrap and refrigerate all day or overnight.

Skewer meat and broil over charcoal fire 20 to 25 minutes or bake in oven at 375° F. about 40 minutes. Baste often with olive oil or butter.

Note: This goes well with a rice pilaf and spinach salad.

Pâté Americain

Elaine Corn
The Courier-Journal, Louisville, KY
The French call it pâté. We call it meat loaf—ugh!

Makes 12 servings

Filling

1 garlic clove, minced
1 tiny onion, minced
8 mushrooms, coarsely chopped
1 tablespoon vegetable oil
1-1/2 pounds ground beef
1/2 pound ground pork
1/2 pound bulk sausage
1-1/2 cups fresh bread crumbs
2 eggs
2 teaspoons salt

4 leaves fresh sage, minced, or
  1/2 teaspoon dried sage
1 teaspoon summer savory
1 teaspoon minced fresh thyme
  or 1/2 teaspoon dried thyme
2 tablespoons chopped fresh
  parsley
1/2 teaspoon ground cumin
1/2 teaspoon black pepper

Dough

10 sheets phyllo dough
1/2 cup butter, melted

3/4 cup fresh bread crumbs

Filling: Sauté garlic, onion and mushrooms in oil until softened. Mash beef, pork and sausage with bread crumbs, eggs, salt, sage, savory, thyme, parsley, cumin and pepper. Add sautéed vegetables. Continue mashing until mixture is very smooth.

Mound mixture in round cake pan, 8 or 9 inches in diameter. Bake in 350°F. oven 1 hour. Drain off as much fat as possible. Cool. Drain again. Leave in pan until ready to wrap with dough.

Dough: Lay first sheet of phyllo dough on buttered cookie sheet. Stroke butter on dough with pastry brush; dust with bread crumbs. Lay next sheet of phyllo over, but slightly askew, as if forming a pinwheel. Repeat with butter and bread crumbs. Continue layering phyllo in pinwheel design with butter and bread crumbs until all sheets are used.

Unmold meat. Place in center of dough. Carefully pull up ends of dough to form topknot or flower design. Generously brush ends and surface with butter. Finish baking, on cookie sheet, in 375°F. oven 20 to 30 minutes, or until crust is golden. Slice after cooling.

Paella

Christine Arpe Gang
The Commercial Appeal, Memphis, TN

*I like to serve paella buffet-style for a crowd. It feeds
a big group and seems more special than most chicken
and rice casseroles.*

Makes 8 to 10 servings

1/4 cup olive oil
1 pound chicken breasts, boned
  and cut into large pieces
1 pound chicken thighs, boned
1 meaty pork chop, diced
1 medium onion, sliced
1 clove garlic, chopped
4 cups chicken broth or stock
1-1/2 cups uncooked rice
  (preferably Spanish or
  Italian rice)
1 can (16 ounces) tomatoes,
  undrained

2 teaspoons salt
1 tablespoon paprika
1/2 teaspoon pepper
1/8 teaspoon saffron
1/2 teaspoon cayenne
1 pound cleaned and peeled
  raw shrimp
2 pounds cleaned mussels or
  clams
1 package (10 ounces) frozen
  peas
1 jar (2 ounces) sliced pimentos

Heat oil in Dutch oven or large paella pan until hot. Brown chicken
and pork about 15 minutes. Remove meat from pan.

Preheat oven to 350°F. Add onion and garlic to fat in pan and cook
until onion is tender. Drain fat. Stir in chicken broth, rice, tomatoes,
salt, paprika, pepper, saffron and cayenne. Add chicken and pork to
rice mixture and heat to boiling. Bake uncovered in oven 20 minutes.

Remove from oven, stir in shrimp and tuck mussels into rice with
opening-side up. Stir in peas. Bake 10 to 15 minutes longer, or until
mussels open and shrimp are cooked. Garnish with pimiento.

No-Noodle Spaghetti

Bev Bennett

Chicago Sun-Times, Chicago, IL

Mother Nature has a good ploy for the pasta-crazed dieter. It's called spaghetti squash. It can be boiled or baked, but I prefer baking. The "spaghetti" will remain a mystery until the squash is cut.

Makes 2 servings

1 small spaghetti squash
1 small onion
6 to 8 large fresh basil leaves or
  1 teaspoon dried crushed
  leaves

2 tablespoons olive oil
2 ripe tomatoes, cored and
  chopped
Salt and pepper to taste
Grated Parmesan cheese

Preheat oven to 350°F. Place spaghetti squash on cookie sheet and bake in oven 1 hour, or until fork pierces skin with relative ease.

Meanwhile, peel and chop onion. Mince basil leaves. Heat olive oil in medium-size skillet. Add onion and basil, sauté 5 minutes. Add tomatoes and simmer another 10 minutes. Season to taste with salt and pepper. (The sauce will taste milder when mixed with the squash.) Remove from heat and set aside.

When squash is tender, remove from oven. Use pot holder or towel to hold hot squash; cut squash vertically in two. Scoop out seeds and dark yellow pulp; run fork along inside squash flesh — it will separate into spaghetti-like strands. Keep working with fork until skin is reached. Repeat with second half.

Spoon spaghetti squash into skillet with tomato sauce. Toss over moderate heat briefly to heat through. Taste and adjust seasonings, if necessary. Sprinkle about 2 tablespoons grated Parmesan cheese on each helping before serving.

Vegetables

Mother's Scalloped Potatoes

Karen K. Marshall

St. Louis Globe-Democrat, St. Louis, MO

My mother makes wonderful scalloped potatoes, so when I decided to do a food page featuring potatoes, I thought Mom's recipe should be included. And I thought a simple long-distance phone call home would do it. "Oh, my," she said. "There is no recipe. I just make them. My Aunt Mary taught my mother and she taught me, but, of course, we've all made changes over the years." I suggested we make them, hypothetically, right then, over the phone. "How many potatoes?" I asked. "What pan are we using?" came her reply. Twenty minutes and a hefty phone bill later, we thought we had it figured out. "If it works," Mom said, "would you send me the recipe?" It took two tries to get enough "oh, medium, I guess" white sauce "to cover the potatoes," but here it is.

Makes 8 servings

5 to 6 medium to large potatoes
1/3 cup all-purpose flour
2 tablespoons butter
2 cups milk

3/4 pound processed cheese spread or 3/4 pound longhorn cheese, chopped or shredded
1 jar (4 ounces) pimientos, drained and chopped
Salt and pepper to taste

Peel and cook potatoes in boiling, salted water. Cool slightly; dice coarsely and set aside.

Make white sauce by combining flour and melted butter in saucepan to form roux. Slowly stir in milk. Continue to stir, cooking over low heat until sauce thickens.

Mix sauce with potatoes and stir in cheese, mixing until cheese melts. Blend in pimientos. Check for seasoning. Pour into 13x9x2-inch shallow baking dish and bake in 350°F. oven 30 to 40 minutes, or until top bubbles and browns slightly.

Okra Gumbo

Clara Eschmann
The Macon Telegraph and News, Macon, GA

Makes 6 servings

4 cups diced okra
3 well-ripened medium
  tomatoes
3 strips bacon

2 small onions, finely chopped
1 green pepper, finely chopped
1 clove garlic, minced
Salt and pepper to taste

Wash okra, cut crosswise and dice fine. Peel tomatoes and chop fine. Fry bacon in skillet until crisp; remove bacon, drain and crumble.

Put okra, onions, green pepper and garlic into skillet with bacon drippings and cook until just tender. Add tomatoes; cook slowly, covered, about 30 minutes, stirring frequently. When done, season to taste with salt and pepper. Sprinkle with bacon and serve.

Note: This is delicious served over toast points or fluffy steamed rice, or in a small bowl as accompaniment to an entrée.

Broccoli-Tomato Casserole

Janet Beighle French
The Plain Dealer, Cleveland, OH

This casserole was shared by Frida Gustafson, a long-time Cleveland caterer. It has been a holiday favorite because preparation is done ahead.

Makes 8 to 10 servings

3 packages (10 ounces each)
  frozen broccoli, thawed and
  drained
3 large fresh tomatoes, peeled
  and sliced (1 quart)

2 cups mayonnaise
1 can (3 ounces) grated
  Parmesan cheese
  (approx. 2/3 cup)

Arrange broccoli in 10-inch round, buttered casserole. Top with tomato slices. Combine mayonnaise and Parmesan cheese, reserving a little cheese to sprinkle on top. Spread mayonnaise mixture over tomato slices and sprinkle with reserved cheese. Cover and refrigerate until ready to bake.

Preheat oven to 325°F. Bake casserole, uncovered, 50 to 60 minutes, or until nicely browned.

Candied Carrots

Charlotte Hansen
The Jamestown Sun, Jamestown, ND

The cranberry glaze in this recipe gives a butter-scotch flavor that is delightful.

Makes 4 servings

5 medium carrots
1/4 cup butter
1/4 cup canned jellied cranberry
  sauce

2 tablespoons light brown sugar
1/2 teaspoon salt

Scrape carrots and slice crosswise on bias about 1/2-inch thick. Cook, covered, in small amount of boiling water, until just tender, 6 to 10 minutes.

Combine butter, cranberry sauce, brown sugar and salt in skillet. Heat slowly and stir until cranberry sauce melts. Add drained carrots; heat, stirring occasionally, until nicely glazed on all sides, about 5 minutes.

Dilled Cucumbers

Claire Barriger
Free-lance writer, Ottawa, Ontario, Canada

These cucumbers taste especially good with roast turkey or chicken

Makes 6 servings

2 cucumbers (8 inches each),
  peeled
2 tablespoons butter or
  margarine
2 tablespoons all-purpose flour

3/4 cup half-and-half
2 tablespoons dried dill weed
1 teaspoon granulated sugar
1/2 teaspoon salt
Dash white pepper

Cut peeled cucumbers in half lengthwise and scrape out seeds with spoon. Cut cucumbers in 1/2-inch cubes. Sauté in butter in large, heavy pan until tender but still firm, about 2 minutes. Sprinkle with flour and stir to blend. Add half-and-half, dill, sugar, salt and pepper. Cook over moderate heat until thickened, stirring constantly. If serving is delayed and sauce becomes too thick, add a little more cream.

Carrot Soufflé

Rosemary Black
The Record, Hackensack, NJ

This is a delicious and easy dish that even carrot-haters will eat.

Makes 4 to 6 servings

1 pound carrots, cooked
3 eggs
1/3 cup granulated sugar
2 tablespoons all-purpose flour
1 teaspoon baking powder

1 teaspoon vanilla extract
1/2 cup butter, melted
Dash ground nutmeg
Dash ground cinnamon

Topping
1/4 cup corn flake crumbs
3 tablespoons light brown sugar

2 tablespoons butter
1/4 cup chopped nuts

Preheat oven to 350°F. Purée cooked carrots in blender. Add eggs to puréed mixture and blend well. Add sugar, flour, baking powder, vanilla, butter, nutmeg and cinnamon. Purée until smooth. Pour into greased 1-1/2-quart soufflé dish.

Topping: Combine crumbs, brown sugar, butter and nuts. Sprinkle over casserole. Bake in oven 1 hour.

Corn Custard

Claire Barriger
Free-lance writer, Ottawa, Ontario, Canada

Makes 6 servings

2 cups fresh or canned corn
  kernels, drained
1/4 cup all-purpose flour
1 teaspoon granulated sugar
1 teaspoon salt

1/4 teaspoon pepper
3 eggs, well beaten
2 cups milk
2 tablespoons butter or
  margarine, melted

Combine corn with flour, sugar, salt and pepper in bowl. Stir in eggs, milk and butter. Spoon or pour into 6 buttered custard cups or 1-1/2-quart casserole. Set in pan of hot water and bake in 350°F. oven for 45 minutes for custard cups, or 1 hour for casserole, or until knife inserted in center comes out clean. Individual custards can be unmolded, if desired.

Carrots, Ginger and Cumin

Marian Burros
The New York Times, New York, NY

Makes 4 to 6 servings

1 pound carrots
6 tablespoons butter, divided
2 teaspoons cumin seed
1 tablespoon chopped fresh
  ginger

2 cloves garlic, chopped
2 tablespoons lemon juice
1/2 cup low-fat or regular milk
Salt and freshly ground pepper
  to taste

Scrape carrots and cut into medium slices, or slice in food processor. Cook carrots in boiling, salted water until just tender, about 5 minutes, depending on thickness of carrots. Drain and rinse under cold water to stop cooking.

Meanwhile, in pan melt 1 tablespoon butter and sauté cumin about 30 seconds. Add ginger and garlic and saute 1 minute longer. Combine cooked drained carrots with cumin-garlic mixture, lemon juice, remaining butter and milk.

Process in blender or food processor with steel blade, in batches, until smooth. Season with salt and freshly ground pepper. To serve, heat through.

Carrots The Good Way

Deni Hamilton
The Courier-Journal, Louisville, KY

I've met lots of people who don't eat cooked carrots unless they are in a stew. For some reason, they like raw carrots, but not cooked. This is one recipe I've found that everybody likes. And I'm especially pleased with it because there's no sugar in it.

Makes 4 servings

1 pound carrots, sliced in 1/4-inch rounds
2 tablespoons horseradish (Do not use horseradish sauce)
1 small onion, finely chopped
1/2 teaspoon salt
Pinch pepper
1/2 cup mayonnaise
1/4 cup dried fine bread crumbs
2 tablespoons butter, melted

Place carrots in saucepan with just enough water to cover; simmer until just tender. Drain well, but reserve about 1/4 cup cooking liquid. Mix reserved cooking liquid with horseradish, onion, salt, pepper and mayonnaise.

Arrange carrots evenly over bottom of buttered 9-inch pie plate. Pour horseradish mixture over carrots. Mix bread crumbs with butter and sprinkle over top. Bake in 375°F. oven 20 minutes, or until crumbs are nicely browned.

Corn Pudding

Barbara Gibbs Ostmann
St. Louis Post-Dispatch, St. Louis, MO

Given to me by my friend Susan Manlin Katzman at a recipe shower when I was married, this delicious vegetable dish has been a favorite ever since. I usually include it on the Thanksgiving table. It is so sweet it could almost be a dessert. When made with fresh corn from the garden, it is out of this world.

Makes 6 to 8 servings

1/2 cup butter
1/4 cup granulated sugar
3 tablespoons all-purpose flour
1/2 cup evaporated milk
2 eggs, beaten

1-1/2 teaspoons baking powder
2 packages (10 ounces each) frozen whole kernel corn, thawed

Preheat oven to 350°F. Melt butter in saucepan. Mix sugar and flour; stir into melted butter. Stir in milk, eggs and baking powder. Mix well. Stir in corn. Pour mixture into 2-quart buttered casserole or two l-quart baking dishes. (I usually make it in two dishes and freeze one for later). Bake in oven until top is golden brown and center is set, about 45 minutes.

Note: This recipe can be prepared in the microwave oven, as well. I melt the butter, then cook the finished dish on high (100 percent) power about 10 to 15 minutes. It will not brown, but will have a great fresh taste. If I am going to freeze it, I only cook it partially, so it will finish cooking when I reheat it.

Fettucine Florentine

Jane Milza
Staten Island Advance, Staten Island, NY

Makes 4 to 6 servings

1/2 cup butter
1 pound fresh spinach or 1 package (10 ounces) frozen spinach, cooked and chopped
3/4 pound bacon, cooked crisp, drained and crumbled
1/4 pound prosciutto or smoked ham, chopped (optional)

2 eggs, beaten
1/2 to 3/4 cup freshly grated Parmesan cheese
1-1/2 to 2 cups heavy cream
1 pound fettucine, cooked al dente
Salt and pepper, if needed

Melt butter in large pot. Add spinach, bacon and prosciutto or ham; mix well and heat. Meanwhile, combine eggs, cheese and cream in small bowl.

When spinach-bacon mixture is hot, add fettucine and mix thoroughly to coat all strands. Add egg mixture and heat, stirring constantly, until slightly thickened. Do not boil. Adjust seasoning, if necessary. Add additional cream if mixture is too dry. Serve immediately.

Golden Stuffed Baked Potatoes

Donna Lee

The Providence Journal and Bulletin, Providence, RI

The color and crunch of grated carrots in these baked potatoes make them unusual.

4 baked potatoes
1 cup grated raw carrots
1/4 cup chopped fresh parsley
1/4 cup minced onion or chives
1/2 teaspoon horseradish
2/3 cup plain yogurt or sour
  cream

1/4 cup melted butter or
  margarine
Salt and pepper to taste
Grated Parmesan or Cheddar
  cheese
Paprika

Halve baked potatoes and scoop out pulp. Whip pulp with carrots, parsley, chives, horseradish, yogurt and butter. Season to taste with salt and pepper. Refill potato halves. Top with grated cheese and paprika. Bake in 350°F. oven 15 minutes, or until cheese melts and mixture is hot.

If desired, filled potato halves can be refrigerated. When ready to serve, remove from refrigerator and top with cheese and paprika. Bake in 350°F. oven 20 to 25 minutes, or until hot.

Greek Style Pilaf

Marge Hanley
Indianapolis News, Indianapolis, IN

Makes 6 to 8 servings

1/2 cup butter
6 green onions, chopped
1 cup sliced fresh mushrooms
3/4 cup uncooked brown rice
3/4 cup orzo (Greek pasta
 product)
3 cups chicken stock

Generous pinch of dried
 oregano to taste
Salt and freshly ground black
 pepper to taste
1 tablespoon chopped fresh
 parsley
1/2 cup pine nuts

Melt butter in large, heavy saucepan over moderate heat. Add onions and cook until soft. Stir in mushrooms and cook until lightly browned. Stir in rice and orzo. Cook several minutes, stirring occasionally, until well coated with butter mixture. Stir in stock, cover and bring to boil. Reduce heat to very low and cook until rice is tender and liquid has been absorbed, 40 to 50 minutes. Mixture will hold well if necessary

Add oregano, salt (depends upon seasoning in stock) and generous amount of pepper, stirring well. Stir in parsley and pine nuts. Remove from heat, or hold over very low heat several minutes to blend flavors.

Marinated Carrots

Harriett Aldridge
Arkansas Gazette, Little Rock, AR

This is nice for a covered-dish supper or buffet dinner.

Makes 6 to 8 servings

2 pounds carrots
1/2 to 3/4 cup granulated sugar
1/2 cup vegetable oil
1/2 cup white vinegar
1 can (8 ounces) tomato sauce

1/2 can (6 ounces) tomato cocktail
1 onion, sliced and separated into rings
1 green pepper, thinly sliced

Scrape carrots; slice and cook in boiling water until tender-crisp. Drain. Combine sugar, oil, vinegar, tomato sauce and tomato cocktail; mix until sugar is dissolved. Pour over cooked carrots, onion rings and pepper slices in large bowl. Marinate in refrigerator for several hours, or overnight.

Pete's Grits Casserole

Evelyn Wavpotich
Island Packet, Hilton Head Island, SC

I always like getting recipes from male cooks. Pete Peterson, a retired pilot, omitted salt from his grits recipe purposely. He, along with so many others, is trying to limit his salt intake. There are many grits recipes, but this one is special.

Makes 6 servings

4 cups water
1 cup quick-cooking grits
1-1/2 cups shredded sharp
  Cheddar cheese

1/2 cup butter or margarine
1/2 cup milk
3 eggs, well beaten
2 to 3 cloves garlic, minced

Preheat oven to 350°F. Bring water to boil in medium-size saucepan. Add grits; return to boil. Reduce heat and cook for 5 minutes, stirring occasionally. Add cheese, butter, milk, eggs and garlic, stirring until cheese is melted, about 5 minutes more. Pour into lightly greased 2-quart casserole or baking dish. Bake in oven 1 hour.

Mashed Potato Stuffing

Linda Giuca

The Hartford Courant, Hartford, CT

This mashed potato stuffing recipe is my family's traditional Thanksgiving stuffing recipe. We've always referred to it as stuffing, although I can't ever remember it used for stuffing the turkey.

Makes 6 to 8 servings

6 medium potatoes
1 pound sweet or spicy Italian sausage
1/2 cup butter
2/3 cup milk (approx.)
2/3 cup shredded American cheese

1/3 cup grated Parmesan cheese
Turkey giblets, cooked and chopped (optional)
2 eggs
Chopped parsley
Salt and pepper to taste

Wash potatoes, pare and remove blemishes. Cook in boiling water until tender. While potatoes are cooking, fry sausage in skillet until thoroughly cooked. Remove sausage from pan and cool slightly. Slice sausage into 1/2-inch rounds and then into quarters; set aside.

Mash potatoes, mixing in butter and milk. Add cheeses, stirring well. Add sausage bits and chopped, cooked turkey giblets, if desired, and mix well. Beat eggs well and blend into potato mixture. Add parsley, salt and pepper to taste. If cheeses are especially salty, omit extra salt. (The consistency of the mixture should be smooth and slightly loose, like a thick pudding. If mixture seems too thick, thin slightly with more milk.)

Pour into greased 1-1/2-quart casserole and bake in 350°F. oven 30 minutes, or until stuffing is set and top is nicely browned.

Potato Casserole Au Gratin

Sue Dawson
Columbus Dispatch, Columbus, OH

I've had lots of requests for this recipe. Our congressman's wife liked it so much that she put it in "The Congressional Club Cook Book."

Makes 10-12 servings

6 medium potatoes
1/4 cup butter or margarine
1/4 cup all-purpose flour
1 cup chicken broth
1/3 cup light cream or
half-and-half
1-1/4 teaspoons salt, divided
Dash pepper
1/2 cup finely chopped celery

1/3 cup finely chopped onion
1/4 cup chopped pimiento,
drained
1 cup grated Cheddar cheese
1/2 cup butter or margarine,
melted
1 carton (8 ounces) sour cream
1/2 cup corn flake crumbs

Boil potatoes with jackets on until almost tender, about 15 minutes. Drain and let cool.

Melt 1/4 cup butter in saucepan. Stir in flour. Slowly add chicken broth and cook, stirring constantly, until mixture thickens and is bubbly. Stir in cream, 1/4 teaspoon salt and pepper. Remove from heat, cover and let cool.

Peel and grate potatoes. Combine with celery, onion, pimiento, cheese, melted butter and remaining salt. Stir in sour cream, then fold sauce into grated potato mixture. Turn into 9x13x2 inch baking dish. Sprinkle with corn flake crumbs. (Casserole can be refrigerated at this point, if desired.) Bake in 325°F. oven for 1 hour.

Potatoes with Mustard and Curry

Vicki Fitzgerald
The Patriot Ledger, Quincy, MA

Makes 6 servings

1/4 cup butter or margarine
6 medium potatoes, cooked and
cut in quarters
1 green pepper, finely chopped

2 medium onions, finely
chopped
1/2 teaspoon curry powder
1/2 teaspoon dry mustard
Salt and pepper to taste

Melt butter in large skillet; add potatoes, green pepper and onions. Sprinkle with curry powder, mustard, salt and pepper; toss to mix well. Fry gently, turning often until potatoes are well browned.

Rosemary Parsnip Casserole

Kathleen Kelly
Wichita Eagle-Beacon, Wichita, KS

Makes 6 to 8 servings

12 parsnips (approx. 2 pounds)
2 tablespoons butter
1/4 teaspoon fresh or dried
rosemary
2 tablespoons all-purpose flour

1/4 cup grated Parmesan cheese
2 cups light cream or
half-and-half
1/2 cup cracker crumbs
1/4 cup melted butter

Peel parsnips. Cook in boiling, salted water until tender. Drain and cut each in half lengthwise, or slice in rounds if parsnips are large. Arrange half the parsnips in bottom of greased 1-1/2-quart baking dish. Dot with half the butter, sprinkle with half the rosemary, flour and cheese. Drizzle with half the cream. Repeat layers. Mix cracker crumbs with melted butter and sprinkle over casserole. Bake, uncovered, in 400°F. oven for 20 minutes.

Ratatouille

Gail Perrin
The Boston Globe, Boston, MA

I like this version of ratatouille because it is layered rather than "scrambled." It also cooks in the oven rather than on top of the stove. This is a good party dish that can be made ahead of time and refrigerated for several days.

Makes 4 to 6 servings

1 medium summer squash, cubed
1 medium zucchini, cubed
1-1/2 teaspoons salt
3 large cloves garlic, mashed or minced
1/3 cup olive oil
2 cups peeled, cubed eggplant
1/2 teaspoon oregano
3 medium onions, thinly sliced
2 medium green peppers, cut into thin strips
1/2 teaspoon dried marjoram
4 medium firm-ripe tomatoes, peeled and thinly sliced
1/4 teaspoon dill seed

Butter 2-1/2-quart casserole. Cover bottom with cubes of unpeeled summer squash and zucchini. Sprinkle with one-third the salt, garlic and oil. Add layer of eggplant, again adding one-third salt, garlic and oil; add oregano. Add layer of onion slices and layer of green pepper. Sprinkle with remaining salt, garlic and oil; add marjoram. Cover casserole and bake in 350°F. oven for 45 minutes. Remove from oven and add layer of tomato slices; sprinkle with dill seeds. Continue baking, uncovered, for 10 minutes. Serve hot or chilled.

Skillet Cabbage

Charlotte Hansen
The Jamestown Sun, Jamestown, ND

Makes 6 servings

4 cups shredded cabbage
1 green pepper, diced
2 cups diced celery
2 large onions, sliced

2 tomatoes, chopped, or 1 can
   (16 ounces) stewed tomatoes
1/4 cup bacon drippings
2 teaspoons granulated sugar
Salt and pepper to taste

Combine cabbage, green pepper, celery, onions, tomatoes, drippings, sugar, salt and pepper in large, covered skillet. Cook, covered, over moderate heat about 30 minutes.

Spicy Minced Watercress

Carol Haddix
Chicago Tribune, Chicago, IL

This makes a nice accompaniment to shrimp.

Makes 4 servings

2 bunches watercress, minced
1 teaspoon salt
3 tablespoons vegetable oil

1 large, dried red chili pepper
2 teaspoons sesame oil

Rinse watercress in cold water; shake dry. Mince both leaves and stems. Put minced watercress in bowl, sprinkle with salt and toss well. Refrigerate 30 minutes. Squeeze dry.

Heat large skillet over high heat until hot; add oil, swirl and turn heat to medium low. Brown chili pepper in oil about 40 seconds, flipping and pressing. Turn heat to high, scatter in watercress and stir-fry rapidly with scooping motions for 30 seconds. Add sesame oil, give a few sweeping turns and pour into serving dish. Refrigerate until watercress is thoroughly cold.

Spaghetti Primavera

Susan Manlin Katzman
Free-lance writer, St. Louis, MO

Spaghetti Primavera is a lush and lovely dish to serve as a first course at a splendid dinner, or as a main course at a wonderful lunch.

Makes 4 to 6 servings

1 cup sliced zucchini
Salt
2 tomatoes, peeled and chopped
3 tablespoons olive oil, divided
3 cloves garlic, mashed, divided
Salt and pepper to taste
10 fresh mushrooms, sliced
8 tablespoons butter, divided
1-1/2 cups broccoli pieces,
  blanched

1-1/2 cups snow peas, blanched
6 asparagus stalks, blanched
  and sliced
1 pound spaghetti, uncooked
1 cup heavy cream, warmed
Chopped basil to taste
  (fresh, if available)
1/2 cup grated Parmesan cheese
Chopped parsley
Sautéed whole cherry tomatoes

Put zucchini in colander and sprinkle with salt. Set aside 20 minutes. Rinse with cold running water and drain. Pat dry with paper towels.

Sauté chopped tomatoes in 1 tablespoon oil with 1 mashed garlic clove, salt and pepper, until tomatoes render their juice.

In another pan, lightly sauté mushrooms with remaining garlic in 2 tablespoons butter and remaining oil. Add zucchini, broccoli, snow peas and asparagus; cook only until heated through.

Cook spaghetti al dente and drain. Melt remaining butter. Toss spaghetti with butter and warm cream. Add basil, salt and pepper to taste. Toss with cheese and vegetables. Sprinkle with parsley. Garnish with cherry tomatoes.

Spinach Casserole

Rosemary Black
The Record, Hackensack, NJ

Three of my seven sisters are vegetarians, and this quick spinach casserole has become a standing item on our Thanksgiving table and at other family dinners. It's nutritious enough to be a main dish, but it's equally good as a vegetable accompaniment. My two-year-old daughter loves it.

Makes 4 to 6 servings

2 eggs, well beaten
6 tablespoons all-purpose flour
1 package (10 ounces) frozen
   chopped spinach, thawed

1-1/2 cups cottage cheese
1-1/2 cups grated Cheddar
   cheese
1/2 teaspoon salt

Preheat oven to 350°F. Beat eggs and flour in bowl until smooth. Stir in spinach, cottage cheese, Cheddar cheese and salt; mix well. Pour into greased 1-quart casserole. Bake in oven for 1 hour.

Squash and Tomatoes
Anne Byrn Phillips
The Atlanta Journal-Constitution, Atlanta, GA

Makes 8 servings

1/2 pound bacon, coarsely diced
3 large onions, cut in half and
    sliced in thin moons
2 green peppers, cut in half and
    coarsely diced
1 cup chopped parsley, divided
1/4 cup chopped fresh basil or
    2 teaspoons dried basil

7 ripe tomatoes, peeled, seeded
    and chopped
10 to 12 small yellow squash,
    trimmed and diced
Salt and freshly ground pepper
    to taste

Place bacon in large, heavy skillet and heat. When half-cooked, stir in onion and green pepper; let sizzle about 3 minutes. Add 1/2 cup parsley, basil, tomatoes, squash, salt and pepper. Cook, stirring and tossing until squash is tender-crisp but not mushy. Garnish with remaining parsley.

Squash Puff
Claire Barriger
Free-lance writer, Ottawa, Ontario, Canada

Serve this casserole with ham or sausage.

Makes 6 servings

3 cups mashed cooked winter
    squash (approx. 4 pounds)
1/2 cup chopped onion
2 tablespoons butter or
    margarine
2 eggs, beaten

1/4 cup light cream or
    half-and-half
3 tablespoons all-purpose flour
1 teaspoon baking powder
3/4 teaspoon salt
Dash pepper
1/3 cup buttered bread crumbs

Cook squash; mash. Sauté onion in butter until transparent. Add to squash. Beat in eggs and cream, then stir in flour, baking powder, salt and pepper. Turn into greased 1-1/2-quart baking dish and top with crumbs. Bake in 375°F. oven 25 minutes, or until lightly browned.

Stir-Fry Brown Rice with Vegetables

Barbara Gibbs Ostmann
St. Louis Post-Dispatch, St. Louis, MO

This recipe was one of the "year's favorite" recipes for our food section. Leftovers reheat well in a microwave oven, making this a perfect dish to tote to the office for lunch. Sometimes I make it just as described, but usually I throw in water chestnuts or vary the vegetables according to what I have on hand. This provides a lot of "chew" satisfaction for dieters.

Makes 4 to 6 servings

1 cup brown rice, uncooked
1 tablespoon chicken bouillon granules
3 tablespoons vegetable oil, divided
1 cup thinly sliced carrots
3 green onions (including some tops), sliced
1 medium clove garlic, minced, or dash of garlic powder
1 large green pepper, sliced in thin strips
1 cup thinly sliced zucchini
1 cup thinly sliced fresh mushrooms
1/2 cup slivered almonds
4 to 5 tablespoons soy sauce

The day or morning before serving, cook rice according to package directions, adding chicken bouillon granules to water. Cool rice completely in refrigerator.

Heat about 1 tablespoon oil in wok or skillet over high heat. Add carrots; stir 1 minute. Add onions, garlic and green pepper; stir-fry 1 minute, adding more oil as needed to prevent sticking. Add zucchini, mushrooms and almonds; stir-fry for about 2 minutes, or until all vegetables are barely crisp-tender. Add rice and stir to separate grains and heat through. Season to taste with soy sauce. Serve at once.

Note: Do not omit slivered almonds. Canned mushrooms may be substituted for fresh mushrooms, if necessary.

Sweet Potato Casserole

Barbara Gibbs Ostmann
St. Louis Post-Dispatch, St. Louis, MO

A good friend, Sidney Fiquette, brought this sweet potato casserole to a potluck picnic at our house a few years ago, and I fell in love with it. She said it was just something her family had always made. I have added it to the Thanksgiving menu, and sometimes sneak it in for other occasions. It is too sweet to serve often. In fact, you could argue in favor of serving it for dessert instead of as a vegetable.

Makes 8 to 10 servings

3 cups cooked mashed sweet potato

1 cup granulated sugar

1/4 cup butter or margarine, softened

1/4 teaspoon salt

1/2 cup evaporated milk

Topping

3/4 cup light brown sugar

1/4 cup all-purpose flour

1/4 cup butter or margarine, softened

1 cup pecan halves

Combine mashed sweet potatoes, sugar, butter, salt and evaporated milk, mixing until creamy. Turn mixture into buttered 1-1/2-quart casserole.

Topping: Combine brown sugar, flour, butter and pecans.

Crumble mixture by hand and spread over casserole. Bake in 350°F. oven for 45 minutes.

Note: You can use canned sweet potatoes and mash them, but it is best when made with fresh sweet potatoes that have been baked and mashed. Chopped pecans can be used, but pecan halves make it more special.

Sweet Potato Balls

Diane Wiggins
St. Louis Globe-Democrat, St. Louis, MO

This recipe is good with holiday fare like baked ham or roast turkey. You can make it weeks in advance, freeze it, then simply place it in the oven 20 minutes before serving time.

Makes 8 servings

3 cups cooked yams or sweet potatoes
1/4 cup butter or margarine
3/4 cup light brown sugar
2 tablespoons milk
1/4 teaspoon salt

1/2 to 1 teaspoon grated orange rind
8 regular-size marshmallows
1 cup corn flakes, crushed, or 1 cup ground pecans

Mash sweet potatoes. Add butter, sugar, milk, salt and orange rind. Scoop up about 1/4 cup potato mixture with tablespoon, and shape mixture around each marshmallow, using more as needed to cover. Roll each ball in crushed corn flakes or ground nuts. Place potato balls in buttered baking dish, cover with foil and freeze.

When ready to serve, preheat oven to 350°F. Take balls directly from freezer, place on pan and put in preheated oven. (Thawing them will make them soggy.) Bake 20 minutes, or until marshmallows begins to ooze.

The Potato Pancake Principle

Joan Nathan
Free-lance writer, Chevy Chase, MD

Recently, when demonstrating how to make potato latkes for Hanukkah, I discarded my recipes and put together a ratio of potatoes to other ingredients. I call it the "potato pancake principle."

Makes 8 to 10 pancakes

2 medium unpeeled baking potatoes (or 1 potato and 1 beet or 1 zucchini)
1 medium onion
2 eggs
Salt and freshly ground pepper to taste
1 handful fresh parsley, diced
1/2 cup (approx.) matzo meal
Vegetable oil for frying
Sour cream or applesauce (optional)

Cut potatoes (or potato and beet or zucchini) and onion into eighths; grate in food processor. Combine grated vegetables with eggs, salt, pepper and parsley. Add enough matzo meal to hold mixture together.

Shape 2 tablespoons potato mixture with hands to make each pancake. Fry pancakes, a few at a time in 1/2 inch hot oil, in heavy skillet. When brown, turn and fry on other side. Drain well. Serve pancakes with sour cream or applesauce, if desired.

Note: I recommend making the pancakes early in the day, letting them drain all day long (do not refrigerate), then crisping them again just before eating. To crisp pancakes, place them on ungreased cookie sheet in 350°F. oven until just warm.

Breads

Aunt Ruth's Cinnamon Rolls

Karen K. Marshall

St Louis Globe-Democrat, St. Louis, MO

These rolls are really good. My Aunt Ruth back in Indiana got the recipe from a friend years ago.

Makes 100 small rolls

2 packages active dry yeast
1/4 cup warm water
2 cups milk, scalded
1 cup granulated sugar
2 teaspoons salt
1 cup (or more) margarine, divided
3 eggs, beaten

6 to 8 cups all-purpose flour
Cinnamon sugar (1 teaspoon cinnamon per cup granulated sugar)
Confectioners sugar icing (confectioners sugar plus enough water to moisten)

Mix yeast with warm water, stirring to dissolve; set aside. Scald milk in small saucepan and mix in granulated sugar, salt and 1/2 cup margarine until sugar is dissolved. Pour into large bowl and set aside to cool. When milk mixture is barely lukewarm, add yeast mixture and stir well. Add eggs and mix well. Add flour, a cup at a time, until dough is firm enough to turn onto well-floured board.

Knead until dough is smooth and satiny. Place kneaded dough in large, greased bowl and turn to grease top. Cover with clean towel and set aside in warm place to rise. When dough has almost doubled, punch down, cover again and let rise a second time.

Melt remaining margarine. Pinch off pieces of dough and roll into balls about the size of ping pong balls. Dip each ball into melted margarine and then into cinnamon sugar. (Don't skimp on margarine or sugar.) Making approximately 100 rolls, place balls, not quite touching, in baking pans. Allow to rise again, 10 to 15 minutes.

Preheat oven to 375°F. Bake 15 to 20 minutes, or until golden brown. While rolls are still warm, drizzle confectioners sugar icing over rolls.

Note: I use disposable foil pans, each holding 15 to 18 rolls. The rolls freeze beautifully after baking, and the foil pans are ideal for this.

These are good served cool, but they are even better warm. They can be reheated in preheated oven at 350°F. for about 5 minutes, or in a microwave oven on medium power for 2 minutes.

Danish Kringler

Lou Pappas

The Peninsula Times Tribune, Palo Alto, CA

In Denmark the holiday bread is often pretzel shaped.

Makes 1 coffee cake

6 tablespoons butter, softened
1-1/2 cups all-purpose flour, divided
1/2 package active dry yeast
2 tablespoons warm water
1/4 cup light cream or half-and-half

Almond Paste Filling
1/2 cup almond paste
2 tablespoons butter

1 egg
2 tablespoons granulated sugar
1/4 teaspoon salt
1 egg white, lightly beaten
Granulated sugar for topping
2 tablespoons sliced almonds

1 egg white
1/4 cup shortbread or sugar cookie crumbs

Beat butter and 2 tablespoons flour until blended. With spatula, spread it into 8x4-inch rectangle on sheet of wax paper and chill. Sprinkle yeast into warm water in large mixing bowl and let stand until dissolved. Heat cream until warm, not hot, and add to yeast. Mix in egg, sugar and salt. Beat until smooth. Gradually add remaining flour and beat until smooth.

Turn out on lightly floured board and knead until smooth and satiny. Roll out into 8-inch square. Place chilled butter mixture in center of dough. Remove paper. Fold dough over chilled mixture from both sides, then fold in thirds. Roll out into 12x6-inch rectangle. Repeat folding and rolling twice. Wrap in wax paper and chill 30 minutes. Roll into 24x6-inch rectangle.

Almond Paste Filling: Beat almond paste, butter, egg white and crumbs until well mixed.

Spread Almond Paste Filling down center of dough. Fold dough from each side to cover it. Place on lightly greased baking sheet and shape into pretzel. Flatten lightly with rolling pin. Cover with towel and let rise at room temperature until doubled.

Preheat oven to 375°F. Brush top of kringler with egg white. Sprinkle with sugar and sliced almonds. Bake 20 to 25 minutes, or until golden brown.

Irish-American Treacle Bread

Peggy Daum

The Milwaukee Journal, Milwaukee,WI

In Ireland, bread means soda bread. And there are probably as many variations as there were black iron pots hanging over turf fires in cottage kitchens. The bread that baked in those pots was, basically, a mixture of flour, salt, baking soda and buttermilk. Some cooks added a little sugar, others added a little butter. A tablespoon or two of flakemeal (rolled oats) varied the texture. Often, some of the white flour was replaced with whole meal (whole wheat flour). Sometimes, to make a fancier loaf, raisins, dried currants, nuts or caraway seeds were added. Treacle bread is a slightly sweet version of soda bread often baked for children. The Irish use the word treacle for what we call molasses. The bread is best sliced thin and served with butter. This recipe evolved from several others. It's similar to some but identical to none.

Makes 1 loaf

3 cups sifted all-purpose flour
1 teaspoon salt
1 tablespoon granulated sugar
1 scant teaspoon baking soda
3/4 teaspoon baking powder

1 cup whole wheat flour
1/2 cup molasses
1 cup (approx.) buttermilk, divided

Sift flour, salt, sugar, baking soda and baking powder in large bowl. Thoroughly mix in whole wheat flour. Warm molasses slightly. Combine with 1/2 cup buttermilk. Make a well in center of flour mixture and stir in molasses-buttermilk mixture. Mix in remaining buttermilk, adding more or less than 1/2 cup as necessary to make soft dough.

Turn out on floured board and knead a few times — only enough to shape into ball. (Use a little additional flour on hands and board if dough sticks.) Flatten to about 1-1/2 inches in thickness. Place in greased and floured 8- or 9-inch round layer cake pan (dough does not have to fill pan). Cut cross at least 3/8 inch deep in top of dough, extending cross down sides. (This is more than traditional decoration; it will help bread to rise and bake evenly and will discourage cracking.) If desired, brush top with additional buttermilk.

Preheat oven to 375°F. and bake bread 40 to 45 minutes, or until bread is browned and pan sounds hollow when tapped on bottom. Remove from pan and cool on rack. Slice thin, toast if desired, and serve with butter.

Note: If you prefer not to sift all-purpose flour before sifting with other dry ingredients, more buttermilk may be needed to make soft dough.

Mother's Corn Bread

Ann McDuffie
The Tampa Tribune, Tampa, FL

My mother made the world's best corn bread, the kind Southerners used to call egg bread. She never measured ingredients. For twenty years I tried to learn how to make it. I even gave her quantities of premeasured ingredients, then measured what was left over and figured how much she used. She started with buttermilk, stirring in leavening until it "sounded right." Then she added other ingredients. I never knew what she meant by "sounded right." And I never mastered her recipe. But after years of trial and error I came up with this recipe that my sisters say is as good as mother's.

Makes 6 to 8 servings

3 tablespoons butter
1 cup cornmeal
1/2 cup all-purpose flour
2 teaspoons baking powder
1/2 teaspoon salt
1 tablespoon granulated sugar
2 eggs
1 cup milk

Melt butter in heavy iron skillet in oven while it is being preheated to 350°F. Combine cornmeal, flour, baking powder, salt and sugar in mixing bowl. Beat eggs; add milk and 2 tablespoons melted butter from skillet. Quickly stir milk mixture into cornmeal mixture. Pour batter into remaining butter in hot skillet. Bake 20 to 25 minutes. Serve hot with lots of butter.

Grandma's Graham Bread
Gail Perrin
The Boston Globe, Boston, MA

Makes 2 loaves

1 package active dry yeast
1/2 cup warm water
1 quart water or milk
1 cup molasses

2 teaspoons salt
8 cups graham or whole wheat
  flour

Dissolve yeast in warm water. Combine water or milk and molasses, then warm them. Pour into large bowl and add yeast mixture, salt and graham or whole wheat flour. Stir well and set in cool place overnight.

In morning, stir well again. Mixture will be runny. Pour into 2 greased 9x5x3-inch loaf pans and let rise 1 hour in warm place.

Preheat oven to 450°F. Bake bread 10 minutes; lower heat to 400°F. and bake about 50 minutes more, or until done. (Sometimes it takes a bit less than full time.)

Osage Squaw Bread
Ivy Coffey
El Reno Tribune, El Reno, OK

Makes 6 servings

4 cups all-purpose flour
2 teaspoons salt
1 tablespoon plus 1 teaspoon
  baking powder

1 tablespoon solid shortening,
  melted
2 cups lukewarm milk
Fat or oil for deep-frying

Sift flour, salt and baking powder into bowl. Stir in shortening and milk. Knead lightly to gather dough into ball. Roll out dough on lightly floured board. Cut into 2-inch squares.

Heat fat or oil in deep fryer to 370°F. Fry 2 or 3 at a time until golden on both sides. Drain on paper towels.

Note: Indians dip the bread in "sop," a mixture of corn syrup and bacon drippings.

Joe's Garlic Bread

Joe Crea

Florida Times-Union, Jacksonville, FL

This is a standard in my recipe repertoire. I haven't had any leftovers yet. Purchase the best Italian or French bread you can find. The bread can be prepared ahead and frozen.

Butter and margarine, softened (approx. 1 cup per loaf)
Garlic cloves, peeled and minced (2 to 3 per loaf)
Honey (optional)

1 loaf (or more) Italian or French bread
Basil
Paprika
Olive oil

Blend softened butter and margarine (half and half, or any proportion desired) with minced garlic. If you wish, beat in a tablespoon or two of honey.

Slice bread in half lengthwise. Spread butter-garlic mixture thickly on both cut sides of bread. Sprinkle lightly with basil, then paprika. Coat outside of loaf lightly with olive oil. Close up.

Preheat oven to 350°F. Wrap loaves in foil and bake in oven 20 minutes, or until inside of bread is hot and garlic is soft. Slice in large hunks and serve hot.

More informally, allow guests to rip off hunks according to appetite. This goes well with lasagna.

Note: If you plan to make garlic bread ahead and freeze it, be sure to ask at the bakery for plastic bags large enough to store the loaves. Wrap loaves in a double thickness of aluminum foil; seal completely and fit back into the plastic bags.

Bake frozen loaves at 350°F. about 30 minutes. Remove from foil, raise temperature to 375°F. Return bread to oven to crisp.

Mother's Molasses Raisin Rye Bread

Eleanor Ostman
St. Paul Pioneer Press and Dispatch, St. Paul, MN

My mother invented this bread by drawing on several Scandinavian recipes. It was an essential at our home during the holidays. After she died, I found a scrap of paper on which I'd written just the ingredients one day early in my marriage. I'd never made the bread while she was alive, but now I've reconstructed the recipe and it tastes just as good as my memories of it.

Makes 3 loaves

2 packages active dry yeast
1/2 cup warm water
3-1/2 cups liquid (milk, water or a combination)
2 cups raisins
2 cups rye flour
1 cup rolled oats

1/4 cup honey
2 tablespoons caraway seeds
5 to 6 cups all-purpose flour
1/2 to 3/4 cup molasses
1/2 cup vegetable oil
4 teaspoons salt

Dissolve yeast in warm water. Combine yeast mixture, liquid, raisins, rye flour, oats, honey and caraway seeds. Add enough all-purpose flour, about 2 cups, to make batter of sponge consistency. Let rise until fluffy.

Stir in molasses, oil and salt. Add enough additional all-purpose flour, 1 cup at a time, to make workable dough. Knead until soft and elastic. Divide dough into three parts. Form into round loaves and place on greased baking sheets. Let rise, covered, in a warm place 1 hour, or until doubled in bulk.

Preheat oven to 375°F. Bake bread 10 minutes, reduce heat to 350°F. and bake an additional 35 to 40 minutes. Cool on wire racks.

Out-Of-This-World Rolls

Donna Morgan

Salt Lake Tribune, Salt Lake City, UT

This is a top favorite at our house.

Makes 2 to 2-1/2 dozen rolls

2 packages active dry yeast
1/4 cup warm water
3 eggs, well beaten
1/2 cup solid shortening
1/2 cup granulated sugar

1 cup warm water
2 teaspoons salt
4-1/2 cups all-purpose flour, divided

Soften yeast in 1/4 cup warm water. Combine eggs, shortening, sugar, softened yeast, remaining warm water, salt and 2-1/2 cups flour. Beat until smooth. Add enough remaining flour to make soft dough. Cover and allow to rise until double. Punch down and place in refrigerator overnight. Three hours before baking, roll out as desired.

Variations: Dinner Rolls—Divide dough in half. Roll each half into rectangle 1/2 inch thick. Spread with butter. Roll up jelly-roll style and cut into 1-inch slices. Place in greased muffin tins, cut side down. Cover and allow to rise 2 to 3 hours.

Preheat oven to 400°F. Bake in oven for 12 to 15 minutes.

Orange Rolls—Combine 1/3 cup melted butter, 1/2 cup granulated sugar and grated zest of 1 orange. Spread on dough instead of butter. Continue preparation as for dinner rolls. Frost with confectioners sugar icing while hot. To make icing: combine 1 cup confectioners sugar and 1/4 to 1/3 cup milk.

Garlic Parmesan Rolls—Pinch off small pieces of dough and roll between hands to make slender sticks. Place on greased baking sheet, brush with melted butter and sprinkle lightly with garlic salt and heavily with Parmesan cheese. Allow to rise and bake as for dinner rolls.

Sour Cream Yeast Rolls

Betty Straughan
The News Review, Roseburg, OR

*When I have guests for dinner, I often serve these
great sour cream yeast rolls. Leftovers, if any, freeze
beautifully. Men love them.*

Makes 72 bite-size rolls

1 package active dry yeast
1/4 cup warm water
2 cups sour cream

2 tablespoons granulated sugar
1/4 teaspoon baking soda
5-1/2 cups biscuit mix, divided

Soften yeast in water. Let stand while combining sour cream, sugar
and baking soda in large bowl. Add 2 cups biscuit mix, then yeast
mixture. Mix well. Stir in 3 more cups biscuit mix. Turn dough onto
board dusted with 1/2 cup biscuit mix. Knead to form smooth ball.

Shape dough into small rounds the size of a walnut. Place close
together in buttered 9x13x2-inch pan. Let rise until doubled in bulk.

Preheat oven to 375°F. Bake rolls 15 minutes, or until done.

Note: Rolls can be made ahead of time and frozen. When ready to
serve, thaw rolls and reheat in oven at 200°F.

Swope Bread

Janet Beighle French
The Plain Dealer, Cleveland, OH

This Swope Bread recipe was printed in a Tacoma, Washington, paper with the explanation that a local skier had picked up the recipe "in the Tyrol." My mother clipped it and discovered she had a family favorite. The bread tastes like far more than the limited number of ingredients. We printed it, and readers of European extraction declared it was indeed "just like something from the old country!"

Makes 2 loaves

4 cups unsifted graham or whole wheat flour
2 cups unsifted all-purpose flour
1 cup granulated sugar

2 teaspoons salt
1 quart buttermilk (or 3-1/2 cups milk acidified with 1/2 cup vinegar)
2 teaspoons baking soda

Preheat oven to 375°F. Grease two 9x5x3-inch loaf pans. Combine both flours, sugar and salt. Combine buttermilk and baking soda; stir into flour mixture. Turn into prepared loaf pans.

Place in oven. Turn down heat to 350°F. Bake 1 hour and 10 minutes, or until done in center when tested with toothpick. Remove from pans and cool on rack.

Whole Wheat Cranberry Bran Bread

Donna Lee

The Providence Journal and Bulletin, Providence, RI

Years after the first harvest festival of 1621 at Plimoth Plantation, Priscilla Alden was asked what she cooked. It's said that she replied, "I don't rightly recall whether we had cranberries. I do love them and all, but my mind was on other things. I'm not even sure we had turkey." Today in New England, we can't imagine a Thanksgiving without cranberries. This bread is a delicious way to use them. It's dark and moist, like bran muffins.

Makes 1 loaf

1 cup all-purpose flour
2 cups whole wheat flour
1/2 cup all-bran or crushed bran
  cereal with raisins
3/4 cup light brown sugar
1 teaspoon baking powder
1 teaspoon baking soda
1 cup chopped nuts

1 cup cranberries, chopped
1/4 cup granulated sugar
1 egg
1/2 cup milk
1/2 cup orange juice
1/2 cup melted margarine or
  vegetable oil

Combine flours, bran cereal, brown sugar, baking powder, baking soda and nuts; mix well. Combine cranberries and granulated sugar. Stir sugared cranberries, egg, milk, orange juice and margarine into flour mixture all at once but only until mixed. Pour into greased 9x5x3-inch loaf pan. Preheat oven to 350°F. Bake in oven 60 to 70 minutes, or until firm in center. Cool in pan 10 minutes, remove to rack and cool on long side before slicing. Freezes well.

Note: One-half cup cranberry-orange relish can be substituted for sugared cranberries.

Whole Wheat Honey Bread

Lorrie Guttman
Tallahassee Democrat, Tallahassee, FL

Makes 2 loaves

4 cups whole wheat flour,
  divided
1/2 cup nonfat dry milk
1 tablespoon salt
2 packages active dry yeast

3 cups water
1/2 cup honey
2 tablespoons vegetable oil
4 to 4-1/2 cups all-purpose flour

Combine 3 cups whole wheat flour, nonfat dry milk, salt and yeast in large bowl. Heat water, honey and oil in saucepan over low heat until warm; pour warm liquid over flour mixture. Blend with electric mixer at low speed 1 minute and at medium speed 2 minutes. Add remaining whole wheat flour and blend with mixer. Stir in about 4 cups all-purpose flour by hand.

Turn onto floured board and knead, adding flour as necessary to keep dough from being too sticky, until dough is smooth and elastic (about 5 minutes). Place dough in greased bowl, turning greased side up. Cover and let rise 45 to 60 minutes, until dough is light and doubled in bulk.

Punch down and divide in half. Roll each half into 14x7-inch rectangle. Starting with 7-inch side, roll up jelly-roll fashion. Place each loaf in greased 9x5-inch pan, tucking sides under. Cover loaves; let rise 30 to 45 minutes, or until light. Preheat oven to 375°F. Bake bread 40 to 45 minutes, until loaf sounds hollow when lightly tapped. Remove from pan, cool on wire rack before slicing. Bread slices even better the next day.

Whole Wheat Zucchini Bread

Claire Barriger
Free-lance writer, Ottawa, Ontario, Canada

*This bread is less sweet than most quick breads. The
zucchini adds color and an interesting texture.*

Makes 1 loaf

1 cup sifted all-purpose flour
1-1/2 teaspoons baking powder
1/2 teaspoon baking soda
1/2 teaspoon salt
1 teaspoon ground cinnamon
1/2 teaspoon ground allspice
1 cup whole wheat flour
2 eggs

2/3 cup vegetable oil
1/4 cup honey
1/2 teaspoon lemon extract
1-1/2 cups shredded zucchini
1/2 cup chopped nuts
1/4 cup raisins
1 teaspoon sesame seeds
   (optional)

Sift all-purpose flour, baking powder, baking soda, salt, cinnamon and allspice. Stir in whole wheat flour. Beat eggs, oil, honey and lemon extract with rotary beater until smooth and frothy. Stir in zucchini. Add flour mixture and stir well, but do not beat. Stir in nuts and raisins. Turn into greased 9x5x3-inch loaf pan. Sprinkle with sesame seeds. Bake in 325°F. oven 1 hour, or until toothpick inserted in center comes out clean.

Hawaiian Banana Bread

Betty Straughan
The News Review, Roseburg, OR

As far as I am concerned, this is absolutely the best banana bread recipe I have ever used. It has a much better texture and taste than any I have seen, and a food editor sees a million of them. My family does not consider it Christmas without banana bread for ourselves and some wrapped in foil to give to neighbors and friends. It freezes beautifully. But a warning . . follow the directions exactly or you will not have this beautiful texture and taste.

Makes 2 loaves

2 cups granulated sugar	2-1/2 cups cake flour
1 cup margarine	1 teaspoon salt
6 very ripe bananas, mashed	2 teaspoons baking soda
4 eggs, well beaten	

Cream sugar and margarine. Add bananas and eggs. Sift flour, salt and baking soda three times. Blend flour mixture into banana mixture. Do not overmix. Turn batter into 2 greased 9x5x3-inch loaf pans.

Preheat oven to 350°F. Bake bread for 55 minutes, or until toothpick tests dry in center of loaf. Turn out immediately to cool on wire rack.

Homemade Sandwich Buns

Joyce Rosencrans
The Cincinnati Post, Cincinnati, OH

Guests expect to taste the unusual from a food editor's table, and home kitchen-testing can involve anything from buffalo meat to shark, yellow Finnish potatoes to cactus. But once in a while, I enjoy serving everyday ordinary foods in novel ways. A big hit, for instance, at summer picnics is the deluxe ham sandwich. Heat a fully cooked ham in a covered grill with damp (hickory or apple) wood chips for that extra-special flavor. Then tuck thin slices of ham inside homemade sandwich buns. Slather with homemade herbed mayonnaise and add a little coarsely ground Pommery mustard, plus homemade pickle chips or sour little French cornichons. These buns are great for beginning bread-bakers because there's no worry about forming the perfect loaf.

Makes 12 buns

3 tablespoons butter
1 small onion, minced
1/2 cup plain yogurt or
 sour cream
1/2 cup water
3 to 3-1/2 cups all-purpose flour,
 divided

1 tablespoon toasted
 wheat germ
1 teaspoon granulated sugar
1 teaspoon salt
1 package active dry yeast
1 egg, at room temperature
1 cup shredded natural
 Swiss cheese

Melt butter and sauté onion in small saucepan until tender but not browned. Add yogurt and water; blend well and heat until very warm, nearly 120°F.

Meanwhile, blend 3/4 cup flour, wheat germ, sugar, salt and dry yeast in large mixer bowl. Add warm liquids and blend quickly with spatula into dry ingredients. Mix at low speed with mixer to blend further, gradually increasing mixer speed. Beat 2 minutes at medium speed, scraping sides of bowl frequently. Add egg, 1/2 cup additional flour and shredded cheese. Beat at high speed 2 minutes; stir in enough additional flour (about 2 cups) by hand to make soft dough. Turn out and knead on lightly floured surface for 8 to 10 minutes, or until smooth and elastic. Place in clean, greased bowl and turn dough to grease top. Cover and let rise 1 hour, or until double in bulk.

Punch down dough and divide into 12 equal pieces. Smooth into ball shapes and space balls well apart on large, greased 15x10-inch baking sheet. Flatten each ball to make bun shapes. Cover loosely with plastic wrap and let rise 1 hour or more.

Preheat oven to 375°F.

Bake buns 12 to 15 minutes. Remove buns from sheet, cool slightly and split to fill as desired.

Herb Butter-Spread Bread

Susan Manlin Katzman
Free-lance writer, St. Louis, MO

If Omar Khayyam had tasted Herb Butter-Spread Bread, his idea of paradise would never have been: a loaf of bread, a jug of wine and thou. The bread would have been enough.

Makes 6 to 8 servings

1 loaf (16 ounces) white bread, unsliced
3/4 cup unsalted butter, softened
1/2 teaspoon salt
1/2 teaspoon Worcestershire sauce
1/2 teaspoon whole-leaf dried thyme
1/2 teaspoon whole-leaf dried marjoram

With serrated-edge knife, cut off top, side and end crusts of bread. Do not cut away bottom crust. Cut bread, leaving bottom attached, in half lengthwise and into 3/4-inch pieces crosswise.

Cream butter. Add salt and Worcestershire. Place thyme and marjoram leaves in palm of hand and crush lightly to release flavoring oils. Add herbs to butter and mix well. Spread all cut surfaces of bread inside and out with butter.

Place bread on rimmed baking sheet. (The butter will run as it heats.) Bake, uncovered, in 325°F. oven about 30 minutes, or until crisp. Serve hot.

Ice Box English Tea Muffins

Donna Morgan
Salt Lake Tribune, Salt Lake City, UT

This is an old family recipe we treasure.

Makes 1 dozen muffins

3/4 cup granulated sugar
1/2 cup butter
1 egg, beaten
1/2 teaspoon salt
1/4 teaspoon ground cinnamon

2 teaspoons baking powder
2 cups all-purpose flour
1 cup milk
3/4 cup raisins

Topping
1/2 cup light brown sugar
1 teaspoon ground cinnamon

1/4 cup chopped pecans

Preheat oven to 350°F. Cream sugar and butter. Add beaten egg; blend well. Combine salt, cinnamon, baking powder and flour and add alternately with milk to creamed mixture. Stir in raisins.

Topping: Thoroughly combine sugar, cinnamon and nuts.

Spoon batter into greased muffin cups and sprinkle with topping. Bake 20 minutes, or until done.

Note: If not using batter immediately, cover tightly and store in refrigerator until needed. Batter will keep 3 to 4 weeks.

Pizza Bread

Jeanne Cummins
Noblesville Daily Ledger, Noblesville, IN

This flavored bread is a welcome change from the ho-hum white loaf for sandwiches. It is an exceptional joy used for a grilled cheese sandwich and is really quite nice totally unadorned.

Makes 2 loaves

7 cups bread flour, divided
3 tablespoons granulated sugar
1 teaspoon salt
1 package active dry yeast

4 heaping tablespoons
  well-seasoned spaghetti sauce
2-1/4 cups tomato juice
2 tablespoons butter

Combine 3 cups flour, sugar, salt and yeast in large bowl. Combine spaghetti sauce, tomato juice and butter in small saucepan. Warm mixture to between 120° and 130°F. Add to flour mixture and beat with heavy wooden spoon or electric mixer about 3 minutes. (A heavy-duty mixer with dough hook or a food processor can also be used.)

Gradually add remaining flour until mixture is rather firm; you will have added about 3 more cups flour. Remove to floured surface and knead, adding more flour (about 1 cup) until dough is supple and no longer sticky. (If you are using a heavy-duty mixer or food processor, this step is not necessary.)

Generously butter large bowl and place dough in it, turning to coat all sides. Cover and allow to rise in warm, draft-free place until doubled, 1 to 2 hours.

Punch down dough and divide into 2 parts. Dough will be sticky. Shape into smooth balls; cover and let rest about 10 minutes. Shape into loaves and place in 2 well-buttered 9x5x3-inch loaf pans. Again cover and let rise until doubled, 45 to 60 minutes.

Preheat oven to 375°F. Bake loaves in oven 10 minutes. Reduce heat to 350° and bake 25 to 30 minutes. Bread should sound hollow when tapped with knuckles. Remove from pans and cool on wire racks.

Whole Wheat Bread, Québec Style

Julian Armstrong

The Gazette, Montreal, Québec, Canada

Molasses was a popular sweetener in much of early Québec cooking. Imported from the West Indies, it flavored and colored breads, cakes, pies and cookies. Come springtime, when the maple sap was flowing, maple syrup was often substituted for molasses. A slice of this nutritious and flavorful bread needs no butter. It makes fine morning toast and freezes well.

Makes 2 loaves

1 teaspoon granulated sugar
1/2 cup lukewarm water
  (105° to 115°F.)
2 packages active dry yeast
1/3 cup solid shortening or lard,
  softened

1/3 cup molasses
  (or 1/3 cup maple syrup plus
  1/4 cup light brown sugar)
1 tablespoon salt
1 cup milk, scalded
1 cup cold water
5 cups whole wheat flour
2-1/2 cups all-purpose flour

Dissolve sugar in lukewarm water in small bowl. Sprinkle yeast over water mixture and let stand 10 minutes without stirring.

Cream shortening in large bowl. Blend in molasses, salt and scalded milk. When shortening is melted, add cold water and blend in; then add yeast mixture. Add whole wheat flour, beating in well. Add enough all-purpose flour to make dough you can knead. Knead on floured surface, adding more flour as required, until dough is elastic in texture. Place in greased bowl, grease top of dough, cover with cloth and let rise in warm place until doubled in bulk.

Punch dough down, divide in two. Shape into two loaves and place in greased 9x5x3-inch loaf pans. Grease tops and cover with cloth. Let rise again until doubled in bulk. Bake in preheated 400°F. oven 25 minutes, or until browned and hollow when rapped sharply with knuckles.

Desserts

Bundt Cake

Ann Criswell
Houston Chronicle, Houston, TX

I first had this cake years ago at a benefit coffee at someone's home. One of the hostesses said her cook made it and promised to give me the recipe. It arrived on my doorstep tucked into a Bundt pan as a Christmas present. Although I've made many cakes, I keep coming back to this recipe year-in and year-out. It's also my family's favorite. My daughter makes it better than I do.

2 cups granulated sugar
2 cups all-purpose flour
1 cup margarine, softened
5 eggs, at room temperature

1 tablespoon combined flavorings (1 teaspoon each vanilla extract, almond or lemon extract, or other flavoring as desired)

Preheat oven to 325°F.

Grease Bundt pan generously (even the nonstick ones). Combine sugar, flour, margarine, eggs and flavorings in an electric mixer all at once and beat until smooth, about 10 minutes. Pour into prepared pan. Bake in oven 1 hour, or until cake is done.

Christmas Fruit Balls
Woodene Merriman
Pittsburgh Post-Gazette, Pittsburgh, PA

It wouldn't seem like Chistmas at our house without these Christmas Fruit Balls. The recipe has been in the family so long I can't remember where it originated. Everyone in the family—including the toddlers—can help make them. There's no cooking. No refined sugar. Just grind the ingredients together (in food grinder or food processor) and roll with your hands.

Makes 30 fruit balls

1 cup golden seedless raisins
1 cup dates
1 cup dried apricots
1 cup chopped walnuts

1 teaspoon grated lemon rind
1 teaspoon grated orange rind
Confectioners sugar

Grind raisins, dates, apricots, walnuts and lemon and orange rinds in food grinder or food processor very fine. Mix well. Roll into bite-size balls. Roll in confectioners sugar. Store in covered jar in refrigerator for at least 2 weeks to mellow flavors. Before serving, you may want to coat again with confectioners sugar.

Naked Apple Pie
Charlotte Hansen
The Jamestown Sun, Jamestown, ND

Makes 6 servings

1 egg
1/2 cup all-purpose flour
1 teaspoon baking powder
1/2 cup light brown sugar
1/2 cup granulated sugar
1 teaspoon vanilla extract

Pinch salt
1/2 cup chopped pecans or
    walnuts
2 medium apples, pared and
    chopped

Beat egg. Sift flour and baking powder. Add flour mixture to egg with sugars, vanilla and salt. Add chopped nuts and apples. Spread batter in greased 9-inch pie pan. Bake in 350°F. oven 30 minutes.

German Apple Pancake

Nancy Pappas
The Louisville Times, Louisville, KY

Makes 6 servings

1/2 cup plus 1 tablespoon
  all-purpose flour
1/2 teaspoon baking powder
1/4 teaspoon salt
6 large eggs, separated
1/2 cup light brown sugar
1/2 cup granulated sugar

1/2 cup plus 1 tablespoon milk
2 teaspoons vanilla extract
1/4 cup lemon juice
3 cups peeled, diced apples
1/4 cup butter
1 teaspoon ground cinnamon
1/4 teaspoon ground nutmeg

Combine flour, baking powder and salt in large bowl, set aside. Beat egg whites until foamy, then gradually beat in the sugars, reserving 2 tablespoons of each. Continue beating until whites are stiff. Beat yolks until thickened, then beat in milk and vanilla.

Pour lemon juice over apples. Stir egg yolk mixture into flour mixture. Continue beating until mixture is smooth. Fold in egg whites and apples.

Preheat oven to 375°F.

Melt butter in 12- or 14-inch skillet with oven-proof handle. Pour in pancake mixture, sprinkle with reserved sugars, cinnamon and nutmeg. Bake in oven for 15 minutes, or until set and lightly browned. Cut into wedges and serve immediately. Like a soufflé, this deflates rapidly as it cools.

Butterscotch Brownies

Rosemary Black
The Record, Hackensack, NJ

These rich, buttery brownies studded with chocolate pieces never last long, and they are super-easy to make. I got the recipe from my mother-in-law, who lives in the Adirondacks. She often has a pan of them waiting when we arrive, car-weary from New York City, to visit.

Makes 20 brownies

2 cups light brown sugar
1 cup margarine or solid
   shortening
4 eggs
1 teaspoon vanilla extract

1/2 teaspoon orange extract
   (optional)
2 scant cups all-purpose flour
1 to 2 cups semisweet
   chocolate pieces

Preheat oven to 350°F.

Cream sugar and margarine, then add eggs, one at a time, beating well after each addition. Add vanilla and orange extracts. Add flour and mix well. Stir in chocolate pieces. (Exact amount of chocolate depends on chocolate flavor desired.) Pour batter into greased 9x12x2-inch baking pan. Bake in oven 35 to 45 minutes, or until done. Cool before cutting.

Pumpkin Pie Cheesecake

Jane Baker

The Phoenix Gazette, Phoenix, AZ

I'm a traditionalist when it comes to holiday fare, but this recipe for pumpkin pie has replaced the old-fashioned one I used to prepare.

1 can (16 ounces) pumpkin
2/3 cup light brown sugar
1 teaspoon ground cinnamon
1 teaspoon ground ginger
1/2 teaspoon ground nutmeg
1/2 teaspoon ground cloves
4 eggs, divided
1 cup evaporated milk

2 teaspoons vanilla extract, divided
1 deep dish (9- or 10-inch) unbaked pastry shell
1 package (8 ounces) cream cheese, softened
1/2 cup granulated sugar

Preheat oven to 350°F.

Combine pumpkin, brown sugar, cinnamon, ginger, nutmeg, cloves, 2 slightly beaten eggs, evaporated milk and 1 teaspoon vanilla in large mixing bowl. Pour into 10-inch pastry shell in deep-dish pie pan. Combine cream cheese, granulated sugar, remaining vanilla and 2 slightly beaten eggs in smaller mixing bowl; beat until smooth. Carefully pour cream cheese mixture over pumpkin filling. (You want the cream cheese mixture to stay on top.) Bake in oven 1 hour, or until knife inserted in center comes out clean. Chill before serving.

Note: The flavor improves overnight, so make it a day in advance, if possible.

Saucepan Indians

Kathleen Kelly

Wichita Eagle-Beacon, Wichita, KS

This quick version of brownies bakes up beautifully in a jelly roll pan. I've adapted the recipe to use cocoa, which is less expensive than baking chocolate.

Makes 32 squares

1 cup butter or margarine
3/4 to 1 cup cocoa powder
2 cups granulated sugar
4 eggs
2 teaspoons vanilla extract

1-1/3 cups all-purpose flour
1 teaspoon baking powder
1 teaspoon salt
1 cup chopped walnuts

Melt butter or margarine in large saucepan over low heat. Mix cocoa and sugar; stir into melted butter with wooden spoon. Continue stirring over low heat until ingredients are well blended. Beat in eggs one at a time, beating well after each addition; mix in vanilla.

Preheat oven to 350°F.

Combine flour, baking powder and salt. Add to cocoa mixture and beat to mix thoroughly. Stir in nuts. Spread in 15x10x1-inch jelly roll pan. Bake in oven for 30 minutes, or until top has dull crust and slight imprint remains when touched lightly. Do not overbake. Cool and cut into squares.

Pecan and Peach Upside-Down Cake

Joe Crea

Florida Times-Union, Jacksonville, FL

This upside-down cake is my hands-down favorite to take to a casual gathering. It's savory, rich, honey-sweet and delectable. The cake recipe originally came from James Beard's American Cooking. I adapted it for use in this recipe.

1-l/2 cups butter,divided (Do not use margarine)
1-1/3 cups all-purpose flour
5 eggs
1-1/3 cups granulated sugar
1 teaspoon baking powder
1/4 teaspoon salt

1/2 teaspoon almond extract
1 cup light brown sugar
1/2 cup honey
1 can (30 ounces) peaches, drained and sliced
Maraschino cherries
1/2 to 1 cup chopped pecans

Blend 1 cup butter with flour until well mixed. Beat in eggs, one at a time, then beat in granulated sugar, baking powder, salt and almond extract. Beat mixture until thoroughly combined. Set aside.

Preheat oven to 350°F.

Melt remaining butter in cast-iron frying pan or any other oven-proof skillet measuring at least 9 inches in diameter, but not more than 12 inches. Add brown sugar; mix well. Add honey and blend thoroughly. Remove from heat and arrange peach slices in decorative pattern, using cherries for accent and color. Sprinkle pecans in corners and over tops of peaches. Cover fruit with batter, spreading carefully with spatula to distribute evenly. Allow at least 1-1/2 inches between batter and rim for expansion during baking. Bake in oven 30 minutes, or until toothpick inserted in center comes out clean.

Do not turn over at this time. The cake should be placed on rack and allowed to cool in order to avoid damaging tender cake. When cake is completely cool, invert skillet onto platter or cake dish. The cake is best stored, covered, at room temperature.

Pudding Delight

Helen Wilber Richardson

The Providence Journal and Bulletin, Providence, RI

This is an ancient recipe, but one that I am continually asked for because it is no longer on the cereal box!

Makes 8 servings

1 quart milk
1 cup natural wheat and barley cereal (Grape-Nuts)
4 eggs, beaten

1 cup granulated sugar
Dash salt
1 teaspoon vanilla extract
Ground nutmeg

Warm milk and pour over cereal in bowl. Let stand 15 minutes. Add beaten eggs, sugar, salt and vanilla, mixing very well. Pour into 13x9x2-inch baking dish. Sprinkle nutmeg over top.

Place dish in larger pan with an inch or two of hot water in bottom pan. Bake in 350°F. oven 1 hour, or until custard is set. Test by inserting table knife in center. (It should come out clean when pudding is done.) If not, bake another 5 to 10 minutes. Recipe may be halved for smaller pudding.

Almond Lemon Torte

Joan Nathan
Free-lance writer, Chevy Chase, MD

This is my favorite Passover dessert.

8 eggs, separated
1-1/2 cups granulated sugar
1/4 cup sifted matzo meal
1/2 tablespoon lemon juice
Grated rind of 1/2 lemon

1/4 teaspoon salt
1 tablespoon cold water
1/2 cup ground pecans
1/2 cup ground almonds

Glaze (optional)
1 egg yolk
1/2 cup lemon juice
1/2 cup granulated sugar

Grated rind of 1/2 lemon
1 teaspoon butter or pareve margarine

Beat egg yolks until light. Gradually add sugar and continue beating until eggs are lemon colored. Sift matzo meal and add to yolk mixture. Add lemon juice, lemon rind, salt and water. Fold in ground nuts.

Beat egg whites until stiff. Fold into yolk mixture.

Preheat oven to 325°F.

Grease 9-inch springform pan with butter or margarine and flour with matzo flour. Pour batter into prepared pan. Bake in oven 1 hour, or until toothpick comes out clean

Serve as is, or with a glaze.

Glaze: While Almond Lemon Torte is still in oven, prepare glaze. Beat egg yolk, lemon juice, sugar and lemon rind. Place mixture in saucepan and bring to boil. Boil, stirring constantly until mixture thickens slightly. Stir in butter.

Remove cake from oven and poke holes in top of cake at 1-inch intervals. When cake has cooled slightly, pour glaze over cake while still in pan. Let stand a few minutes so glaze sinks in, then remove cake from pan.

Gingered Pumpkin Slices

Sandal English

Arizona Daily Star, Tucson, AZ

Fresh pumpkin has been rediscovered in the last few years for delights that extend far beyond pies. Next time you prepare fresh pumpkin for steaming, save a portion for this delicious accompaniment to grilled ham or sausage patties for Sunday brunch.

Makes 6 servings

1/4 to 1/3 small round pumpkin
Lemon or lime juice
2 egg whites
1/2 teaspoon ground cinnamon
Margarine or butter

1/2 cup granulated sugar
1/4 teaspoon ground ginger
2 tablespoons finely chopped
   walnuts or almonds

Remove seeds and peel from pumpkin; cut into thin slices. Marinate for 1 hour in lemon or lime juice.

Beat egg whites until foamy; combine with ground cinnamon. Drain each pumpkin slice; dip into egg mixture and sauté in butter until lightly browned. Roll in sugar combined with ginger and nuts.

Fresh Pineapple Pie

Joe Crea

Florida Times-Union, Jacksonville, FL

Fresh pineapple pie probably is one of the best-received recipes we've printed. The nut crust was a wonderful discovery and fits with a number of other pie recipes calling for a graham cracker crust.

1 large, fresh pineapple
1/2 cup granulated sugar
2 tablespoons cornstarch
1 teaspoon freshly grated
  lemon peel

1/8 teaspoon ground nutmeg
1-1/2 cups water
3 drops yellow food coloring

Nut Crust
2/3 cup toasted ground walnuts
3/4 cup vanilla wafer crumbs

1 tablespoon granulated sugar
5 tablespoons butter, melted

Twist crown from pineapple. Cut pineapple into quarters. Remove fruit from shell. Core and cut pineapple into bite-size chunks.

Combine sugar, cornstarch, lemon peel and nutmeg in large saucepan. Stir in water and food coloring. Cook, stirring constantly, until sauce is clear and thickened. Remove from heat. Add pineapple chunks. Cool.

Nut Crust: Toasted walnuts—Preheat oven to 325°F. Grind walnuts; spread in shallow pan. Bake in oven 10 to 15 minutes, or until just roasted, turning occasionally to roast evenly. Advance heat to 400°F.

Vanilla wafer crumbs—Add vanilla wafers, a few at a time, to blender and blend.

Combine walnuts, crumbs, sugar and melted butter. Press into bottom and up sides of 10-inch pie plate. Bake in oven 8 minutes. Cool.

Spoon fruit into cooled crust. Pour sauce evenly over fruit. Cover and chill overnight.

The Ultimate Rice Pudding

Ann Criswell

Houston Chronicle, Houston, TX

This makes the best rice pudding for the least effort of any I've tried.

Makes 4 servings

3 cups milk

1/4 to 1/2 cup granulated sugar

2 cups cooked rice

2 to 3 tablespoons butter

1 teaspoon vanilla extract

Combine milk, sugar, rice and butter in saucepan. Simmer 20 to 30 minutes, or until thick. Remove from heat and stir in vanilla.

Note: You may use the lesser amount of sugar (1/4 cup) and substitute half-and-half for the milk. In case a rice pudding binge leads you to dieting, try the recipe with 1/4 cup granulated sugar substitute and skim milk or skim evaporated milk. It's still super.

Ann's Pastry

Ann McDuffie

The Tampa Tribune, Tampa, FL

This is the best pastry recipe I know. I got it from my friend Ann Kerr, a Tampa attorney and a good cook. We like to cook together and have used this pastry for pies, both fruit and custard; mushroom tarts; and sweet and nonsweet tartlets—it works with all of them.

Makes 9-inch crust

6 tablespoons cold, unsalted butter, cut into small pieces

2 tablespoons solid shortening

1-1/4 cups all-purpose flour

2 tablespoons ice water

Cut butter and shortening into flour until mixture resembles coarse meal. Toss in water and mix until dough forms ball. Knead a few seconds. Refrigerate 1 hour before rolling out.

Mrs. America Chocolate Cake

Cy Meier

Thompson Newspapers of Upper Michigan, Calumet, MI

I received this recipe from a contestant in the Mrs. America Pageant in 1955. I'm not sure what state she represented or if she won the contest, but I do know this cake has been a winner every time it's been served. For all of our birthday celebrations, it's a "must."

3 squares (3 ounces) unsweetened chocolate
1 cup water
1/2 cup butter or margarine
1 teaspoon vanilla extract
2 cups granulated sugar, divided
3 large eggs, separated

2-1/2 cups sifted cake flour
1/2 teaspoon salt
1 cup sour cream
1-1/4 teaspoons baking soda
1 teaspoon red food coloring (optional)
Cocoa for dusting pans

Chocolate Frosting
1/4 cup butter or margarine
2 squares (2 ounces) unsweetened chocolate
Dash salt
1 teaspoon vanilla extract

1 box (16 ounces) confectioners sugar, sifted
5 tablespoons (approx.) evaporated milk

Combine chocolate and water in small saucepan. Bring to boil and cook over low heat until chocolate is melted. Stir to blend. Remove from heat and set aside.

Cream butter, vanilla and 1-1/2 cups sugar until light and fluffy. Add egg yolks and beat well. Sift flour and salt three times. Add to butter mixture alternately with sour cream. Blend well after each addition until smooth.

Sprinkle baking soda over chocolate and blend well. Add to creamed mixture and blend thoroughly. Add red coloring, if desired.

Whip egg whites, which have been warmed to room temperature in nonplastic bowl, until soft peaks are formed. Gradually add remaining sugar, a tablespoon at a time, and continue to beat until stiff, but still shiny, peaks are formed.

Add large spoonful meringue to cake batter and beat in. Add remaining meringue to batter and gently fold in with rubber spatula. Spoon batter evenly into 2 lightly greased and cocoa-dusted round 8- or 9-inch layer pans. Let set in pans 5 minutes before placing in oven. Preheat oven to 350°F.

Bake in oven 40 to 45 minutes, or until cake tests done when toothpick is inserted in middle. Remove from oven and cool in pans 5 minutes before removing to wire rack to cool completely. Frost when cold.

Frosting: Melt butter and chocolate in saucepan over very low heat or in top part of double boiler over hot, not simmering, water. Stir in salt and vanilla. Blend in sugar and enough milk to make smooth, spreading consistency, beating well after each addition.

Frost cake, using about 1/3 the frosting between layers and the rest on sides and top. Store cake in refrigerator until served.

Nutmeg Cake
Kathleen Kelly
Wichita Eagle-Beacon, Wichita, KS

2 cups light brown sugar
2 cups sifted all-purpose flour
1/2 cup margarine
1/2 cup finely chopped almonds, divided

1 cup sour cream
1 teaspoon baking soda
1 egg
1 teaspoon ground nutmeg

Preheat oven to 325°F.

Mix brown sugar, flour and margarine until fine and crumbly. Press one-fourth this mixture into well-greased 8- or 9-inch square pan. Sprinkle with half the almonds. Mix sour cream and baking soda; then mix in egg, remaining crumb mixture and nutmeg; blend well. Pour over mixture in pan. Sprinkle with remaining almonds. Bake in oven 40 to 50 minutes, or until done.

Hot Fudge Pudding

Kathy Lindsley

Rochester Times-Union, Rochester, NY

This was always my favorite dessert as a child. It's my mother's recipe, and although it's easy to make, she always saved it for special occasions—it's very rich! The end result is also something of a miracle, considering how the recipe is put together. It's wonderful hot with whipped cream or with ice cream melting into it, but it's also great cold, the next day, as an indulgence.

Makes 6 servings

1 cup all-purpose flour
2 teaspoons baking powder
6-1/2 tablespoons cocoa powder, divided
1/4 teaspoon salt
1-1/4 cups granulated sugar, divided

1/2 cup milk
2 tablespoons melted butter
1 teaspoon vanilla extract
1 cup chopped nuts (optional)
1/2 cup light brown sugar
1 cup cold water

Sift flour, baking powder, 1-1/2 tablespoons cocoa, salt and 3/4 cup granulated sugar. Stir in milk, melted butter and vanilla. Add nuts. Pour into well-buttered 9-inch square pan. Combine remaining sugars and cocoa. Sprinkle over batter. Pour water over all. Bake in 375°F. oven 45 minutes, or until done.

Poppy Seed Tea Cake

Mary Frances Phillips

San Jose Mercury and News, San Jose, CA

This cake is wonderful for holidays such as Easter, when you don't want an especially sweet dessert. It is nice for serving with tea or coffee, and great for brown bag lunches.

1/3 cup poppy seeds
1 cup buttermilk
1 cup butter or margarine
1-1/2 cups granulated sugar
4 eggs
2-1/2 cups sifted all-purpose
   flour
2 teaspoons baking powder

1 teaspoon baking soda
1/2 teaspoon salt
1 teaspoon orange extract
Cinnamon sugar
   (2 tablespoons granulated
   sugar and 1 teaspoon ground
   cinnamon, thoroughly mixed)

Combine poppy seeds and buttermilk. Refrigerate overnight for full flavor.

Cream butter with sugar until light and fluffy. Add eggs, one at a time, beating after each addition. Sift flour, baking powder, baking soda and salt. Add orange extract to creamed mixture. Blend in flour mixture alternately with poppy seed mixture, beginning and ending with dry ingredients. Turn half the batter into greased and floured 10-inch Bundt or tube pan. Sprinkle cinnamon sugar on top. Add remaining batter. Bake in 350°F. oven 1 hour, or until cake tests done. Cool 10 minutes; remove from pan and finish cooling.

Pioneer Bread Pudding

Dorothy Kincaid
Milwaukee Sentinel, Milwaukee, WI

This bread pudding recipe is just one of the drawing cards at Johnny's Cottage Restaurant in Sister Bay, Wisconsin. Some people have been known to eat it for breakfast, and orders of it go home to Chicago in carry outs. Four or five large pans of the pudding are sold every day.

Makes 4 to 6 servings

2 cups day-old bread cubes (1/4 to 1/2-inch pieces), crusts removed
2 cups milk
1/4 cup granulated sugar

3 tablespoons butter
2 eggs
Dash salt
1/2 teaspoon vanilla extract

Lemon Sauce
1 cup granulated sugar
2 tablespoons cornstarch
1/8 teaspoon salt
2 cups water

1 tablespoon grated lemon peel
1/4 cup butter
2 tablespoons lemon juice

Preheat oven to 350°F.

Place bread cubes in buttered 1-quart baking dish. Combine milk, sugar and butter in saucepan; heat until sugar is dissolved and butter melted. Beat eggs slightly, adding dash of salt. Stir into warm milk mixture and add vanilla. Pour over bread cubes.

Set baking dish in pan of hot water. Bake in oven 1 hour, or until knife comes out clean when inserted in center.

Serve hot or cold with plain cream, or serve hot with lemon sauce.

Lemon Sauce: Combine sugar, cornstarch and salt in saucepan. Stir in water and lemon peel. Boil one minute; remove from heat and stir in butter and lemon juice.

Everyday Cookies

Eleanor Ostman
St. Paul Pioneer Press and Dispatch, St. Paul, MN

"You should enter these in the Minnesota State Fair,"
I told a friend after tasting these sensational cookies.
They're the best I'd ever had. Although she was quite ill
at the time, she took some to the fair and won a ribbon.

Makes 8 to 10 dozen cookies

1 cup butter or margarine
1 cup granulated sugar
1 cup light brown sugar
1 cup vegetable oil
2 eggs
1 teaspoon vanilla extract
3-1/2 cups all-purpose flour

1 teaspoon cream of tartar
1 teaspoon baking soda
1 teaspoon salt
1 cup crispy rice cereal
1 cup quick-cooking oats
1 cup shredded coconut
1/2 cup chopped pecans

Preheat oven to 350°F. Cream butter, sugars and oil. Add eggs and vanilla; beat well so oil doesn't separate. Add flour mixed with cream of tartar, baking soda and salt. Stir in rice cereal, oats, coconut and nuts. Drop by teaspoonfuls onto ungreased cookie sheet; flatten slightly. Bake on lower shelf of oven 5 to 6 minutes.

Move to middle of oven and finish baking until lightly browned, about 5 minutes. Watch carefully so they don't become too brown. Remove from sheets and cool.

(If a pan of cookie dough is ready to put on the lower shelf of the oven when the one already in the oven is moved to middle shelf, baking will be speeded.)

Chocolate Chip Cupcakes

Phyllis Richman
The Washington Post, Washington D.C.

This Chocolate Chip Cupcake recipe was published by the Nestlé company many years ago, and ever since has been one of my standbys. When the recipe was printed in the Post, during the editing process the 1/2 teaspoon baking soda became 1 teaspoon. A more significant error was the illustration – drawing of a high, puffy cupcake, whereas they actually are small and dense – halfway between a cookie and a cake. Our phones lit up with calls from confused readers. When I decided to print the recipe again, I gave the recipe to four people for testing—two used 1/2 teaspoon baking soda and two used 1 teaspoon. Before the testing got underway, a local television station's newscast reporter related the incident on the air, saying the recipe caused toothaches and was a waste of $5.00 worth of ingredients. The reporter claimed the Post was apologizing. Our testing confirmed that there was little difference between the amounts of baking soda. However, I reprinted the original recipe, and the television reporter, this time, apologized. The cupcakes gained countless new fans.

Makes 16 cupcakes

Batter

1/2 cup butter, softened
6 tablespoons granulated sugar
6 tablespoons light brown sugar
1/2 teaspoon vanilla extract

1 egg
1 cup plus 2 tablespoons all-purpose flour
1/2 teaspoon baking soda
1/2 teaspoon salt

Topping

1/2 cup light brown sugar
1 egg
Pinch salt
1 cup (6 ounces) semisweet chocolate pieces

1/2 cup coarsely chopped walnuts
1/2 teaspoon vanilla extract

Preheat oven to 375°F.

Batter: Cream butter, sugars and vanilla. Beat in egg. Sift flour, baking soda and salt; stir into butter-sugar-egg mixture. Spoon by rounded tablespoonfuls into enough paper-lined muffin tins to make 16 cupcakes. Bake in oven 10 to 12 minutes. Remove from oven. While cupcakes are baking, prepare topping.

Topping: Beat brown sugar, egg and salt until thick. Stir in chocolate pieces, nuts and vanilla.

As soon as cupcakes are removed from oven, spoon 1 tablespoon topping over each and immediately return to oven; bake 15 minutes longer. Remove cupcakes from muffin tins at once.

Swedish Cake

Donna Morgan
Salt Lake Tribune, Salt Lake City, UT

This is an old family favorite, which is actually deceiving—no booze!

1 package (16 ounces) raisins	1/2 teaspoon ground cinnamon
3 cups water	1/2 teaspoon ground nutmeg
2 cups granulated sugar	1/2 teaspoon ground cloves
1 cup solid shortening	2 eggs
4 cups all-purpose flour	1 cup chopped nuts
1 teaspoon baking soda	1 teaspoon vanilla extract
1/4 teaspoon salt	

Place raisins, water and sugar in saucepan; bring to boil. Reduce heat and simmer 20 minutes. Add shortening and stir until melted. Cool.

Preheat oven to 350°F. Sift flour, baking soda, salt, cinnamon, nutmeg and cloves in mixing bowl. Add raisin mixture, eggs, chopped nuts and vanilla. Blend well. Pour into greased and lightly floured 13x9x2-inch baking pan. Bake in oven 45 minutes, or until cake tests done.

Ricotta Cassata

Linda Giuca
The Hartford Courant, Hartford, CT

Every Easter, we looked forward to Ricotta Cassata, a deep-dish sweet ricotta pie, which was a specialty of my Sicilian Grandmother. Some recipes call for the addition of golden raisins or tiny pieces of chocolate. Hers has only sugar and cinnamon as flavorings.

Crust

1-1/4 cups all-purpose flour, sifted
l/2 teaspoon salt

1 tablespoon granulated sugar
1/3 cup solid shortening, chilled
1/4 cup cold water

Filling

3 eggs
1-1/2 pounds ricotta cheese
1/4 teaspoon salt

1/4 cup light cream or
   half-and-half
1/2 cup granulated sugar
1 teaspoon ground cinnamon

Crust: Combine flour, salt and sugar in large bowl. Cut in shortening until mixture is crumbly. Sprinkle water, 1 tablespoon at a time, over mixture, mixing quickly with fork until pastry holds together.

Place dough on lightly floured surface; shape gently into ball and flatten. Lightly flour rolling pin and roll dough into large circle. Transfer pastry to 9- or 10-inch pie plate. Make filling.

Filling: Beat eggs in mixing bowl until light and frothy. Beat ricotta in large bowl until smooth; add eggs, salt and cream, beating until smooth.

Preheat oven to 375°F.

Pour mixture into pastry shell and sprinkle top with mixture of sugar and cinnamon. Bake in oven 10 minutes; reduce heat to 350°F. and bake 25 to 30 minutes, or until done.

Abbie's Sugar Cookies

Jann Malone
Richmond Times-Dispatch, Richmond, VA

My Grandmother Abbott always had the dough for these cookies waiting in the freezer for me to cut into Santas, stars and Christmas trees. She didn't seem to mind that I got more of the red and green sugar sprinkles on the floor than on the cookies.

Makes 3 dozen cookies

1/2 cup butter
1 cup granulated sugar
2 eggs
1 teaspoon vanilla extract

1-1/2 cups all-purpose flour
2 teaspoons baking powder
Sugar, nuts, cherries for decoration

Cream butter and add sugar gradually. Add eggs and vanilla; beat until light. Sift flour once before measuring, then sift again with baking powder. Add to butter mixture. Chill the dough.

Preheat oven to 400°F. Roll out dough very thin on floured surface and cut into shapes with cookie cutters. Place on cookie sheets and sprinkle with sugar or decorate with colored sugar sprinkles, nuts and cherries. Bake in oven 10 minutes, watching carefully so they do not burn.

Note: I usually freeze the dough until I'm ready to use it. Then I pull off just enough dough to roll out and cut about a dozen cookies and return the rest to the freezer. Left at room temperature, the dough is very sticky.

Pumpkin Angel Squares

Sue Dawson
Columbus Dispatch, Columbus, OH

Pumpkin Angel Squares might make you think of pumpkin pie. The unmistakable flavor of well-seasoned pumpkin is there. But it sits atop a buttery pecan crust and a layer of fluffy cream cheese. This do-ahead dessert makes a welcome alternative to autumn's favorite pie.

1 cup all-purpose flour
1/2 cup butter or margarine, softened
1/2 cup finely chopped pecans
1 package (8 ounces) cream cheese
3/4 cup granulated sugar, divided
1 cup frozen whipped topping, thawed

1 envelope unflavored gelatin
1/4 cup cold water
1 can (16 ounces) pumpkin
3 eggs, separated
1/2 cup light brown sugar
1/2 cup milk
1-1/2 teaspoons pumpkin pie spice
1/2 teaspoon salt

Preheat oven to 375°F.

Mix flour, butter and pecans with pastry blender until crumbly. Pack into 9-inch square pan. Bake in oven 15 to 20 minutes or until lightly browned. Cool.

Combine cream cheese, 1/2 cup granulated sugar and whipped topping with electric mixer. Spread on cooled crust and chill in refrigerator.

Soften gelatin in water. Combine gelatin mixture with pumpkin, egg yolks, brown sugar, milk, pumpkin pie spice and salt in large saucepan. Cook over moderate heat, stirring, until mixture begins to bubble. Cover and cool.

Beat egg whites until frothy. Slowly add remaining granulated sugar and continue beating until stiff and glossy. Fold into pumpkin mixture. Pour over cream cheese mixture. Chill until set. Cut into squares.

Strawberry-Raspberry Shortcake

Marilyn McDevitt Rubin
The Pittsburgh Press, Pittsburgh, PA

This is the best shortcake I know and the best biscuits ever. During the winter I often make just the biscuits and serve them hot for breakfast with whipped butter and white clover honey.

Makes 6 servings

Shortcake

2 cups all-purpose flour	1/2 cup butter or margarine
4 teaspoons baking powder	2/3 cup light cream or
3 teaspoons granulated sugar,	half-and-half
divided	Additional butter for
1/4 teaspoon salt	assembling

Fruit

l-l/2 quarts fresh strawberries	1 to 2 cups heavy cream,
Granulated sugar to taste	whipped
1 package (10 ounces) frozen	
raspberries	

Shortcake: Sift flour, baking powder, 2 teaspoons sugar and salt. Cut in butter until mixture resembles coarse meal. Stir in cream until dry ingredients are moistened and cling together. Roll or pat out into circle 1 inch thick. Cut into six 2-1/2- to 3-inch circles, shaping scraps to make the necessary number. Sprinkle surface of shortcake biscuits with remaining sugar. Bake on ungreased cookie sheet in 400°F. oven 15 to 18 minutes, or until golden brown. Shortcake biscuits should be served warm. They may be made ahead and reheated at serving time.

Fruit: Strawberries—Wash; reserve 6 of the best for garnish and hull remainder. Slice or leave whole as desired. Sugar as required. Refrigerate. Raspberries—Defrost and extract juices by pressing berries in strainer. Set juice aside in pitcher; discard pulp.

To Assemble: Split and butter warm shortcake biscuits. Distribute half the strawberries over bottoms, cover with top halves and spoon on remaining strawberries. Top with whipped cream, garnish with whole strawberries and pour raspberry sauce over all. Pass extra raspberry sauce in pitcher.

Grandma's Blueberry Butter Cake

Kingsley Belle
The Chronicle, Glens Falls, NY

Nostalgia, for me, lies in an old suitcase full of unorganized recipes scribbled in my grandmother's handwriting. They are not always easy to decipher, but once prepared, they inevitably produce the tastiest gems I have ever eaten. One of her most delectable recipes is this one.

Makes 10 to 12 servings

3 cups all-purpose flour, sifted
1/4 teaspoon salt
3 teaspoons baking powder
2/3 cup butter

1 cup granulated sugar, divided
1 teaspoon vanilla extract
1 cup cold water
4 egg whites

Topping

1 package (8 ounces) cream cheese
3 tablespoons milk
2 tablespoons granulated sugar
1 teaspoon vanilla extract

1 jar (4 ounces) apple jelly
1 pint fresh blueberries
1 cup heavy cream, whipped
2 tablespoons granulated sugar (optional)

Preheat oven to 350°F. Sift flour, salt and baking powder twice. Cream butter and 3/4 cup sugar. Add vanilla to cold water. Alternately combine water and flour mixtures with butter mixture; mix well after each addition. Beat egg whites until stiff, then beat in remaining sugar. Fold egg whites into batter. Pour into well-greased 13x9x2-inch pan. Bake in oven 30 minutes, or until toothpick comes out clean. Prepare topping.

Topping: Beat cream cheese with milk, sugar and vanilla until of spreading consistency. Spread over cooled cake. Melt jelly in saucepan over low heat. When completely melted, remove from heat. Clean berries and add to jelly, tossing lightly until well coated. Be careful not to crush berries. Distribute evenly over cream cheese. Cover entire cake with whipped cream. Cream can be sweetened with granulated sugar if desired.

Index

D

DIP
  curry, 17
  dill, in bread bowl, 18
  lime fruit, 24
  vegetable hot, 34
DRESSINGS
  caper vinaigrette, 49
  soy mayonnaise, for Oriental
    shrimp salad, 54

_____ E

EGGS
  brunch soufflé, 68
  egg-shrimp divine, 24
  spinach frittata, 22
  trail ride (huevos Mexicanos), 75
Eggplant appetizer, 25
Endive, hearts of palm, and
    avocado, 49
English tea muffins, ice box, 126

_____ F

Fall-vegetable soup, cream of, 42
Fettucine Florentine, 93
FISH
  Boston bluefish, baked, 74
  fillets amandine, broiled, 73
  Lake George shrimp (perch), 62
  orange-tuna-macaroni salad, 45
  salmon roll, 30
  sea bass with fennel butter,
    broiled, 69
  smelts in orange sauce, baked, 74
Frankfurters, red devil, 79
Frittata, spinach, 22
Frosting, chocolate, 142

G

Garlic bread, Joe's, 115
Gazpacho, 39
  salad, molded, 50
German apple pancake, 132
German potato salad, 44
German-style venison roast, 63
GINGER
  carrots with cumin and, 90
  pumpkin slices, gingered, 139
Gougère bourguignon, 26
Graham bread, Grandma's, 114
Greek-style pilaf, 95
Grits casserole, Pete's, 96
Gumbo, okra, 87

_____ H-L

Hawaiian banana bread, 123
Hearts of palm, endive, and
    avocado with cape
    vinaigrette, 49
Herb butter-spread bread, 125
Honey bread, whole wheat, 121
Huevos Mexicanos
    (trail ride eggs), 75
Irish-American treacle bread, 112
Joe's garlic bread, 115
Kringler, Danish, 111
Lake George shrimp (perch), 62
LASAGNA
  spinach, 77
  Steve's favorite, 76
Lime fruit dip, 24

_____ M

Marinated carrots, 96
Meatballs, sweet and sour, 32
Meat loaf (pâté Americain), 82